ON THE TURN
OF THE TIDE

MI5
LONDON BLITZ
TURMOIL IN AFRICA
DREAMS, MEDIUMS AND POETRY

THE AUTOBIOGRAPHYOF
DIANA FYNN

GOLDPANNER BOOKS
DEVON
UK

First published in 2005
By Goldpanner Books

This book may be purchased on-line from www.goldpanner.org

A catalogue record for this title is available from the British Library

ISBN 0 9550461-1-4

Printed on recycled paper in Great Britain by Bookchase, London

Goldpanner Books is a division of Eco-nomic Ltd

Eco-nomic Ltd
Edgcumbe House
Bere Ferrers
Yelverton
Devon
PL20 7JL
United Kingdom

Dedication

To the memory of three close South African friends
in the Royal Air Force who all died during 1940 and1941

Hugh Haswell

Claude Goldsmith

Antony Fry

Contents

Preface

The loss of a much-loved elder brother in childhood and later the disappearance of the man I loved, on active service in the RAF at the beginning of the Second World War, precipitated my first psychic experiences and changed my life before I was twenty. I went on to spend three years in MI5 at the height of the war as secretary to Roger Hollis (who was later suspected of being the Fifth Man in the MI5 spy-ring); I married and later had five children; went to Africa and worked with orphans in Southern Rhodesia (now Zimbabwe); co-founded the Centre Party to oppose apartheid and racism in that country, and edited a political newspaper during Ian Smith's regime. Finally my husband and I were forced to leave and on our return to England my life changed dramatically once again. This book tells the story of the 85 years of my life and of the many interesting spiritual and psychic experiences which have illuminated it.

There are many pitfalls to face once you have decided to put your life into a book, one of them being that honesty will compel you to write it as it was. This is hard, because you are not an island, and what you write will inevitably concern others. The realisation of this has been so daunting that it has brought me to a halt in the middle of several chapters. If your book is to be of value, it may eventually express the whole philosophy of your life (something which you may not realise when you embark upon the project). It has to be written in truth, but it must be your own truth and may not be seen in the same way by those who thought they knew you. This you have to accept.

My life began in London and at first followed the normal course expected by my parents. I was educated, 'came out' as a society debutante and was presented at Court, and was trained as a secretary. Because of the war I then entered MI5 in the spring of 1940. After my marriage and the end of the war I endured a nightmare sea voyage from England to South Africa with my first two children, then only babies, to join up with my husband in Southern Rhodesia, where we lived for the next 26 years.

It was not until the 1960's that I first thought that the situation occurring in Rhodesia was worth recording, not as a historian, which I am not, but as a mother. My children were growing up in a disturbed country, and would one day have to make their own choices in attitude. When I have discussed their childhood with my children, some of whom are now grandparents, they have assured me that their memories of Rhodesia have left them with a love of the country and a longing to return. Like me, they recall the smell of the earth when the rains came, the sound of the chorus of insects which one learned to live with, and the high voices of the African people calling across the wide spaces of the countryside. In light of the present situation in Zimbabwe, all this has reverted into a distant dream. I am thankful that a deep love of the real Africa has remained with them and that they do not suffer from the disease of racism which infected so many Rhodesians in this period after the Second World War.

My own memories of Rhodesia are mixed, many of my experiences there being traumatic, some of them challenging, and all of them life-changing. By 1960 I was politically far away from the racist policies of the Rhodesia Front government and its prime minister Ian Smith, so much so that I was one of the founders of the Centre Party. My politics eventually led to my being banned from entering South Africa, which was both an honour and an inconvenience, causing difficulties when we had to leave Rhodesia in 1972.

Our arrival in Britain was followed, eight years later, by the breakup of my marriage, and I began to consider writing a book for my own sake and not just for my children. During the following years in Topsham in Devon, my life changed so much that it often seemed to belong to someone other than myself. I had brought with me from Africa the love of some close friends and together with the help of new-found friends in Topsham I learned that love is a gift which you may only *keep* by giving away. By 'love' I do not mean temporal love, but the love which is outside time. It has been through many friends and experiences that the philosophy of my life has been able to find its way onto these pages.

All the unattributed poetry in the book has been written by me but has often seemed to be inspired by those unknown, or no longer present. These poems and others will one day form another, smaller book. T. S. Eliot defined poetry as 'not the expression of personality, but an escape from personality.' He believed that poetry is the only true way of expressing emotion. I hope that some of the poetry within this book fulfils these criteria, and adds to its deeper meaning.

Raynor C. Johnson wrote two particular books which, amongst many others, have inspired and expanded my awareness of mysticism and spiritual experience. They are *The Imprisoned Splendour* and *Nurslings of Immortality*, reprinted by the Pelegrin Trust. I believe that Raynor will sense my gratitude and love in the dimension in which he now finds himself. I would like to recommend his books to those whose interest has been aroused by the events which have added colour to my life, and which appear in detail in the later chapters of *On the Turn of the Tide*.

My Thanks

Throughout the writing of this book I have been thankful for those friends who have helped and inspired me by adding their thoughts and ideas to mine. However, I must take responsibility for the description of the many spiritual events recorded here, apart from those tape-recorded at the time.

Particular thanks are due to Lily Neal, my dedicated editor, and to Michael Poole, of Goldpanner Books, who has been an enthusiastic and patient publisher.

The Dream of the Pool

I searched for the Self,
which is beyond all searching,
in the depths of a pool left in the rocks
by the receding ocean;
there, in that pool, a reflection of self.
I spoke to the pool and asked it who it was.

 "Are you the ocean which formed you,
the rocks which surround you,
the sunlight which reflects in you,
the creatures which live in you?
Or are you water which lies
in a hollow of rock?"
The pool answered me.
"Wait and watch."

In the long waiting I watched the pool,
I watched the ocean,
I became pool in my understanding.
I felt the reflection of sun,
the movement of creatures in the depths.
I became the coolness of water,
the hardness of rocks,
and I waited.

Time passed.
Ocean crept upon the rocks,
in the darkness of night it overcame pool,
reclaiming that of itself
left amongst rocks on the falling tide.
Pool returned to Ocean exulting, free,
carrying experience into the All
known before birth, one with Ocean,
the All That Is. Yet I, on the dry rocks,
waited and watched.

As dawn broke over the Earth
Ocean receded, pool formed, water in rock.
I said "This is my self, I am this pool,"
but the pool said,
"Wait, watch and listen".

"I am no separate pool. I, an aspect of Ocean,
shall be taken and again made free.
Tide which formed me will reclaim me,
rocks, which gave me form,
will hold a new aspect of Ocean.
That which you have named pool
is form filled by Ocean."

"Consider the reality of pool,
that which is All That Is,
ever changing, ever the same,
past thoughts now one with Ocean.
Born today, a new form of Ocean,
new thoughts on the falling tide
in the evening of time."

I was afraid, I saw myself
without form, an emptiness.
I no longer knew whether I was.
Was I space within the form of my flesh?
Was I no thing, incomprehensible?

Wisdom from Ocean claimed my mind.
"You, ever changing, yet always the same.
As pool desires Ocean, you desire All That Is
into Whom you will be taken,
on the turn of the tide."

Two Brief Family Trees

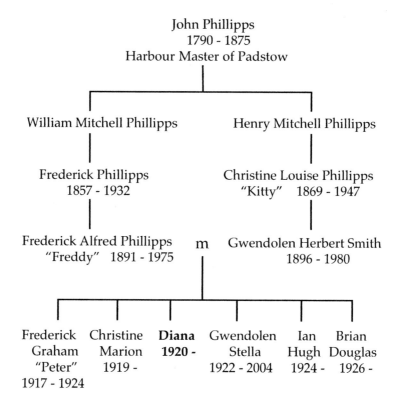

John Phillipps
1790 - 1875
Harbour Master of Padstow

William Mitchell Phillipps

Henry Mitchell Phillipps

Frederick Phillipps
1857 - 1932

Christine Louise Phillipps
"Kitty"   1869 - 1947

Frederick Alfred Phillipps
"Freddy"   1891 - 1975   m   Gwendolen Herbert Smith
1896 - 1980

| Frederick Graham "Peter" 1917 - 1924 | Christine Marion 1919 - | **Diana** **1920 -** | Gwendolen Stella 1922 - 2004 | Ian Hugh 1924 - | Brian Douglas 1926 - |

****

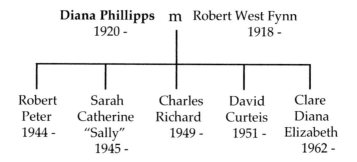

Diana Phillipps   m   Robert West Fynn
1920 -   1918 -

| Robert Peter 1944 - | Sarah Catherine "Sally" 1945 - | Charles Richard 1949 - | David Curteis 1951 - | Clare Diana Elizabeth 1962 - |

Chapter 1

Ancestors

My story begins with John Phillipps, a sea captain, who lived from 1790 to 1875 and who, in later life, became Harbour Master of Padstow in Cornwall. He had two sons, William Mitchell Phillipps, who had a son, Frederick, in 1857, and Henry Mitchell Phillipps who had a daughter, Christine Louise, in 1869.

When Frederick grew up he met and fell in love with his cousin Christine, who was then twenty years old. This caused great trouble in the family as they were first cousins and by the laws of the Church they could not marry. Frederick, deeply distressed at this decision, left England to work as a cattle rancher in Canada, while Christine, usually known as Kitty, married Norman Herbert Smith, a solicitor in the City of London.

Some years later Frederick returned to England and married a girl called Marion Gurney who returned with him to Canada, where they went to live in the north of the country in Portage Le Prairie, which at that time was a remote and lonely area. This must have been difficult for Marion, who had always lived a sheltered life in England. There, in the wilds of the Northern territories, she gave birth to her first child, Freddy. She was terrified and, many years later, she told me that she had had no idea how the baby was to get out of her body, wondering whether her navel would open to enable its arrival. The whole performance horrified her and she had no member of her own family to whom she could turn for help and advice. Bringing up a small child in that wild and desolate country, with no previous knowledge of children, was no easy matter either. For example, on one occasion when, on a winter's night, the family was riding home in a sleigh, two-year-old Freddy dropped one of his gloves in the snow. The scent set wolves on their trail and they were chased for miles in the dark by a howling pack.

However, Freddy survived and at the age of twelve was sent back to England to public school. In the natural course of things he later met Gwendolen, his second cousin, the daughter of his father's cousin Christine and her husband Norman. To the consternation of Freddy's father, history repeated itself, and the two young people fell in love. At first they were prevented from marrying, more because of the enmity between their two fathers than because they were second cousins. However their two mothers got together and after much persuasion the marriage took place, but only after Gwen had passed her twenty-first birthday and no longer required her father's consent. These two lovers, Freddy and Gwen, were my parents.

My father had started to read medicine in London at St. Thomas' Hospital and in August 1914, some years before he married Gwen, but only three or four weeks before the start of the Great War, he had volunteered with some friends from the hospital to serve in the French Horse Ambulance Corps. They went immediately into action. However, by the end of the year it was clear that the war would not be short and all British medical volunteers were asked to return to Britain to complete their medical training. My father did not return to St Thomas' but applied for a commission in the Seaforth Highlanders instead.

He was wounded on July 1st 1916, the first day of the Battle of the Somme. Following an assault by the Rifle Brigade on the German front line he had led his own platoon 'over the top' with orders to take the second line. However, the attack by the Rifle Brigade had failed, with enormous casualties, and he realised that he was leading his men into extreme danger. As the line moved forward men fell around him and he was hit by a bullet which entered the left side of his chest and exited out of his back below his right shoulder-blade. The impact caused him to fall into a bomb crater, in which was another wounded man who was able to staunch my father's wounds. He probably saved my father's life. Although my father was unable to use the upper part of his body and his companion had the use of only one leg, after some hours they managed to help each other back to their own lines. On that day alone 37,000 men were lost. Freddy was eventually sent to a hospital in London, where, as luck would have it, he was nursed by Gwen's sister Molly. He was unable to return to the Front but, after his partial recovery, he was sent as an instructor to a bombing training station.

Freddy and Gwen were eventually married at St. Paul's Knightsbridge on St Valentine's Day, 14th February 1917. After the wedding they went to live in a flat in Battersea in Overstrand Mansions, and at the end of the war my father resumed his medical career at St Thomas' Hospital. In all they were to have six children, Peter, Christine, Diana (myself), Stella, Ian and Brian. Miss Emily Whiddington, our nanny, who came to us when Peter was born, stayed until the youngest child went to prep school. She was the perfect example of an old-fashioned nanny - kind, but strict in her own way - and we all loved her. It was she who carried me into the church on the occasion of my christening, when an elderly nun asked my mother the names of the children. Apparently the nun was horrified at the name given to me and said "How shocking to give your first two children lovely Christian names and the third the name of a heathen goddess!" My mother was upset as she had not considered such a thing for a moment.

The flat where we lived overlooked Battersea Park and was an ideal place for children, four of whom were born within the first seven years of my parents' marriage. Much of our early childhood was spent playing in the wide expanses of the Park, feeding the ducks and geese in the ponds and running along the winding paths. Peter, the object of all my love, was an unusually caring child and I do not recall that he was ever difficult or angry. Although I was only tiny I did everything to please him. I caught greenflies for him, tiny green-winged insects which lived in the cast-iron moulded ends of the seats in the Park, and because my fingers were small and could lift them by their wings without harming them, he allowed me to put them into matchboxes for him.

They were to be kept as pets, but I fear that they died lingering deaths.

When my sister Stella arrived, it must have been quite a tight fit in the flat with my parents, our nanny and four children. I was too young to recall whether there were any other servants, but I feel sure there must have been a cook as my mother lived her whole life without ever learning the art of cookery.

By 1922 my father, who had come top in most of his medical and surgical exams at St. Thomas' Hospital, was a fully qualified doctor. The following year he was asked by Sir Arthur Guinness to take up the post of ship's surgeon on the yacht *Fantome II* on a round-the-world trip, which was expected to take eleven months. He was delighted but my poor mother was dreadfully apprehensive, particularly after she had been to the insurance company to cover his belongings, and had been told that the premiums were very high because private yachts had a tendency to catch fire in mid-Pacific. Strangely enough as things turned out this is exactly what did happen, but somehow the fire was controlled and my father, the Guinness family and the crew members were unharmed.

Fantome II's arrival outside Yokohama coincided with the destructive earthquake of 1923, and the yacht was forced to stand off from the coast until the worst tidal-waves had subsided. The devastation was terrible and bodies were piled in the streets. Many of the houses had been made of paper and had burnt like torches. One of the most distressing things, which remained in my father's memory for many years, was the number of infant girls who had been disposed of in the harbour. At this period in Japan girl children were not rated as highly as boys. The few babies picked up alive by the yacht's crew could only be handed to the sisters-of-mercy at the convents, who were already overwhelmed with homeless children. When I was about eight years old I opened my father's photograph album of the trip and was horrified to see pictures of the piles of corpses in the streets of Yokohama. I felt that I had done something dreadful by looking at the book and so never told anyone. However, about twenty years later the memory returned when I saw the gruesome photos of the dead in Belsen.

I was only three years old but I dimly remember my father's return home eleven months after he had left us. I can picture the dark concrete staircase outside the Battersea flat and the painted banners we had made to welcome him. It is hard to know how much we remember and how much we learn later on, but this is probably a reliable image. I know at least that it is not my earliest memory. I have a clear picture in my mind of standing on tiptoe, holding the edge of a table, trying to see my second birthday cake which loomed huge and white above me with a black china cat sitting on top of it.

Chapter 2

The Death of My Brother

A few months after my father's return from his travels my six-year-old brother Peter was taken ill and died within forty-eight hours. In those days there were no miracle cures for what may have been virus pneumonia, nor was it possible to diagnose his illness at that time. It was providential that my father returned when he did or my mother would have been alone to face the terrible distress of the death of her eldest child.

The loss of Peter made a turning point in my own infant life, for at three and a half I was quite old enough to feel the agony which was overwhelming the family. When Peter's illness became critical, my two sisters, Christine aged five and Stella almost two, our nanny and I had been sent to my maternal grandmother's flat in Ashley Gardens. Nanny and my grandmother were distraught, but we children could not understand what had happened. I recall sitting on my nanny's lap as she wept, and asking again and again what was the matter and crying in sympathy for I knew not what. Perhaps it was explained to Christine but not to me because I was considered too young to understand. However, I remember the fear caught from their weeping and the sense of loss which darkened my life when eventually I realised that Peter had gone for ever.

My distress was, I suppose, not even guessed at by the adults in the family, all of whom were overcome by their own grief. Love comes to us at our birth and is the strongest and most consuming feeling in our earliest years; the sudden disappearance of the one who had meant most to me during my three years cannot be understood by others, but has stayed with me for the rest of my life.

After Peter died we were sent with Nanny to stay with my father's parents, Frederick and Marion Phillipps, who were no longer in Canada. They lived in Jersey in a large house called "Sandybrooke". While we were away my mother and father moved to No. 4 Lower Sloane Street, a large house with eight bedrooms and two bathrooms. Returning to such a huge home after our small flat made a great impression on me.

No. 4 was a very tall building and had an imposing staircase of seventy-seven steps from the hall to the top floor, as well as a stone staircase inside the walls from the basement to the bedroom floor, which was known as 'the servant's stairs'. I believe it was not considered right in those days to meet the maids on the front staircase unless they were working, and they were certainly never seen on the front stairs in their off-duty clothes. There were three maids' bedrooms on the top floor, a bathroom, and another room which had different uses. It served as a bedroom for the governess, when we had one, and later as a studio for us girls, for we were very creative. On the floor below we three girls slept in a large room at the front of the house, while Nanny and the two boys (who were born after the move) occupied a second bedroom along the passage. My parents had made a day nursery out of a third room at the back of the house, overlooking the Duke of York's Headquarters and the long garden which served all the houses on the right-hand side of Lower Sloane Street. There must have been times when I occupied that back room, for I remember nights when I was meant to be sleeping, lying awake listening to the soldiers practising the bagpipes.

The floor below the nurseries had two very large bedrooms, one for my mother and father and one used as a spare room. They had their own bathroom and a separate lavatory with a large mahogany seat, a willow pattern toilet bowl, and a brass handle which had to be pulled up to flush it. We all longed to be allowed to use it (the nursery one not being nearly as special) but this was not permitted except in cases of emergency.

The drawing room and a room called the boudoir were on the first floor and were connected by a wide passage which crossed the stairwell.

The drawing room was very large and had a stone balcony which looked out onto Lower Sloane Street, but I never remember that it was used. The boudoir, which was a small feminine sitting room where my mother could entertain her female friends, faced the long, communal garden at the back. The ground floor hall was tiled in marble and there was a large dining room, a study (used as a consulting room by my father) and a small cloakroom. My father used the dining room as a waiting room, and had set up a huge tropical fish tank on the mantelpiece. He was very fond of his fish and spent almost as much time assisting at the birth of the live offspring of his Siamese fighting fish as he did with the patients in his practice. One day when he was called urgently to an actress who had taken an overdose, he shouted to my mother asking if she knew where his stomach pump was. When she suggested (correctly) that it might be in the fish tank, he snatched it up, ran it under the tap in the cloakroom despite her protests, and rushed off down the Kings Road, calling out as he left the house, "In her state it will make no difference!" She survived.

My father's consulting room, or study, opened onto the garden at the back of the house. We were not often able to use the garden because there was no access to it apart from through the study, and this was forbidden territory. If we did manage to get out we had to stay there, rain or shine, until one patient had gone and before the next was admitted.

A door from the hall led down to the basement and up to the floors above by the stone 'back stairs'. Our knowledge of the basement was limited, for we were not allowed down there for fear of upsetting the cook. There was a servant's hall, a large pantry for Freda and Dorothy, the parlour maid and the housemaid, and a very large kitchen and scullery for Ellen, the cook, and for the kitchen/nursery maid. There was also a bedroom for the cook in the area at the front of the house near the coal-hole where the back steps led up to the street. The nursery maid had to bring meals for the children, Nanny and herself up from the basement kitchens to the nursery floor. They were carried up on a large, black, tin tray and warmed again on a small stove near the nursery.

Whistles connecting all the floors were set into the wall in the passages. When we wanted to alert the kitchen that the nursery was ready for a meal, Nanny had to remove the whistle on our floor and blow hard into the hole in the wall. The whistle in the basement sounded, was then removed and the maid put her ear to the hole to listen to Nanny's orders from above. We children, of course, had other ideas and frequently blew into the hole when Nanny was not looking and then blew into the maid's ear when she put it to the hearing-piece! Of course, this was strictly forbidden and we were punished.

From the night-nursery windows we could look down on the street below. I remember it best with the evening gas lamps shining on a soft London fog, and the the muffin-man's bell sounding as he carried his wares on his head on a covered tray. The lamplighter with his long pole appeared in the evenings to light the gas lamps along the street and around the Square, and there was also 'Friendy', the rotund crossing-sweeper, who had a large family and benefited from our constant supply of second-hand children's clothes. Open-topped buses could be seen from our bedroom windows as they rounded Sloane Square, and on our walks we sometimes passed houses in front of which straw had been laid to silence the noise of the horses' hooves on the road. Nanny told us that this meant that someone was ill or dying within the house and, needless to say, this intrigued us. We tiptoed past with our hands over our mouths for fear of making a noise.

We lived at 4 Lower Sloane Street from 1923 until November 1940, when the house was bombed in the Blitz and my parents were forced to move to a flat in Lowndes Square.

When I was four I was alone at the head of the stairs in the passage which ran between the night and day nurseries. It was evening and the lights were not yet on. Peter came towards me down the passage from the night-nursery and I saw him clearly, wearing the 'grown-up' dressing-gown he had been given for Christmas just before he became ill. He came close to me and smiled, then walked into the bedroom where

Ian, the new baby, was sleeping. I was so excited that I ran downstairs to tell my mother.

'I have seen Peter,' I called to her. 'He has come with us to the new house!' My mother was overcome. She told me that it was not possible, but she was so distressed that I was afraid of what I had done to upset her so badly. I knew that I had seen him and that he had also seen me, but I suddenly understood that such things were secret and not to be told, although they could never be forgotten. It was many years before I was to have another psychic experience, but when it came it changed the course of my life.

Chapter 3

Growing Up

As I grew up the memory of Peter's death turned me into an introverted child. Being in the middle of a large family is never easy, and to be the middle one of three girls makes it even harder. My mother took me with her to see Peter's grave in Brookwood Cemetery on several occasions and also to the grave of her father which was close to Peter's. I think she must have realised that I was the one who missed Peter the most, for my elder sister never came with us. However, I knew that his essential self was not there in the grave, and my childish mind rebelled at the idea of his body lying under all that earth.

I began to distrust my father from the time when Stella and I had our tonsils out at home on the nursery table. I was about six years old and Stella must have been four. Unknown to us preparations were made, and the day-nursery was set up as an operating theatre. Stella and I had both been ill and we were in bed in the night-nursery when my father came in one morning and took Stella away. I asked my governess where she had gone and got no reply. Shortly after this I heard Stella screaming at the far end of the passage. I was told that it was children playing in the street, but I knew my sister's voice and realised that something awful was happening and that people were telling me lies.

Some time later Stella was returned in the arms of my father, anaesthetised and therefore unconscious, but to me she looked dead. I was picked up and taken along to suffer the same fate that she had been subjected to. To add to my fear, the nursery had been changed: the doll's house was shrouded in a white sheet, the furniture was all covered, and three masked figures were grouped round the nursery table. I remember that the room smelled horrible. I screamed in terror as my father forced me onto the table, and my arms and legs were held down by the masked men. Then a white figure placed a suffocating mask over my nose and mouth and I kicked with all my six-year-old might. Suddenly the world started to rotate in black and red circles and there was a roaring in my ears. I heard the voices of the strangers chatting with my father and my last thought was that he was helping them to kill me. It amazes me now that no-one had thought of preparing us for what was to happen. The result of the operation was that Stella and I were extremely ill. We both had high temperatures and serious glandular infections at the bed of the tonsils, and had to lie with our heads held between sandbags for some weeks while the swelling in our necks subsided. There were no antibiotics in those days and little could be done.

After this I began to imagine that Peter's death was the fault of my parents. Perhaps they had not taken proper care of him? This fear was increased many years later when I crept down the passage one night and stood outside the bedroom door of my youngest brother who was screaming. My mother and father were with him and they were angry. I was afraid that they might be going to kill him and yet I could not find the courage to go into the room. Suddenly the screaming ceased and they came out of his bedroom. I fled back to bed and waited to find out whether he was all right. Apparently they had been trying to make him take a pill, but I did not learn this until some time later!

Sadly, I grew up with a deep distrust of my father, although never of my mother. This distrust only began to dwindle in my later years when I realised that he was a kind man who would never harm anyone, but nevertheless I was never close to him.

The joy of leaving London for holidays in the country has always remained in my memory as a highlight of childhood. Norfolk, one of our favourite holiday destinations, lingers as a place of magic where we could roam alone down lanes and into the wet woodlands, where unexpected flowers hid in the hedgerows and nests could be found like treasure in the Spring.

We left London at the beginning of each holiday, five children and sometimes a dog or various other pets. With Nanny Whiddington and the nursery maid we needed a string of taxis to take us to Liverpool Street Station where we boarded a steam train to Wroxham in Norfolk. The packing for five children for a month in the country was accomplished by Nanny, who crammed most of our possessions into the 'clobber bag', a wartime relic belonging to my father. I remember it as a mountainous container which stood in the nursery for a week before our departure, so large that I could not see inside it. As I grew it shrank, but it always retained its evocative smell of wet sand-shoes and bathing towels and the promise of exciting times ahead.

Arriving at Wroxham we were met by the shooting brake from the Hall at Hickling where we always stayed. Set in the midst of its own farmland on the outskirts of the village, the Hall had once belonged to my grandfather, who still retained the shooting around Hickling Broad. The house was large and the Borrett family, who lived there at this period, temporarily moved to the back premises to make room for Nanny, the nursery maid, and us.

To the west of the house were stables originally designed for the farm horses and carriages, but by then sadly occupied by a single pony trap which we used, together with our bicycles, to get to the beach at Sea Palling. Next to the stables were the pigsties and barns and behind the house the cowsheds and dairies. There was no garden as such for playing in, but a large, walled vegetable garden. The pond was always interesting and the barns formed a wonderful playground where we slid down mountains of grain and climbed onto the roof beams.

A wartime friend of my father's named Teddy Barnet became an adopted uncle and fascinated us on many excursions, when we could escape from the watchful eye of Nanny and wander with him into unknown territory. Every lane signposted 'Byroad' (and there are many in that part of the country) led, according to Teddy, to a town or city unknown to all but a few and pronounced 'Bih-roh-ad'. At the age of five

I had complete faith in his knowledge of this magical place and again and again we set off to find it. As each lane came to an end we searched for the next signpost which would direct us on our way, only giving up the search until another day when supper or bedtime intervened. More than eighty years on I still feel the magic of the search and many a time have longed to turn off when driving past such a signpost.

Perhaps Teddy was so good with us because he had the gift of recalling his own childhood, something which other adults seemed unable to do. Whatever the secret of his charm was, however, I know that even when I grew old enough to read and understand the true workaday meaning of the signposts, I never lost the feeling that, somewhere down those unknown paths, if you persisted, you would eventually arrive in Bih-roh-ad. Life has led me down many byroads, through many different experiences, and once or twice I have seen the distant spires of an unknown city or felt the presence of fellow travellers in the search. We are all looking for the City of Meaning which, like a mirage, moves with us, only to be found one day in another dimension.

For two weeks at the end of the summer we went to our grandparents in Jersey. This was a very different sort of holiday, for at Sandybrooke there were garages and stables, two tennis courts, a huge garden with a fountain in the centre of the lawn and several greenhouses. My grandparents had three gardeners, a chauffeur and a number of indoor staff, the chief amongst whom was Clara the cook who made exceptional birthday cakes.

The preliminaries to this holiday were rather more carefully prepared and our clothes were selected to fit the situation. We would be expected to go visiting with my grandmother, but we also spent much time on the beach. We were afraid of my grandfather who was a gruff old man, frequently ill and not very used to children, but my grandmother was sweet-natured and even seemed to enjoy the onslaught on her house. The highlight of the holiday was always a pirate party in St Aubin's Castle which was situated on a rock a little offshore. The castle belonged at that time to Lionel Cox, a great friend of my grandparents. It could be reached by walking across the sands, but depending on the tide we either had to go or return by boat, which added to the enjoyment. Lionel set up a wonderful treasure hunt throughout the dungeons and when we finally found the treasure chest there were presents for all. He would be standing over the chest wearing a sword and the raiment of what may have been a Knight of Malta - very impressive with a great red cross on a white background. I remember him as another beloved adopted uncle.

My happiness in Jersey was marred, however, by the journey to and from the mainland. The boat was small, the sea was always rough and to make matters worse Nanny was a very poor sailor. We embarked from Southampton at night and usually arrived in St Helier at breakfast-time the following morning in an unhappy state, for on many occasions all five of us followed Nanny's example and gave way to seasickness. The greatest achievement was by Stella at the age of about three. Just as we were getting ready to meet my grandmother on the quay she proudly announced, much to Nanny's horror, "I 'ave beed sick in Nana's hat." Poor Nanny. I wonder that she did not give in her notice each year on our return.

The birth of my second brother, Brian, occurred when I was six years old and just the right age to appreciate a new baby. It was felt that Nanny would now have too much to do with five of us, so schooling for the girls was arranged by my mother and over the early years we had a series of governesses who came in the day and taught us in the nursery. It was quite a common practice for parents in those days to assist their impecunious friends by employing them to teach their children. We disliked all of them and Nanny was our staunch supporter in this. She would much rather have been responsible for all five of us. One such 'friend' who taught us the piano destroyed any wish we might have had to learn to play by her frequent use of a ruler on our knuckles. However, a resident governess, Joan Hobbs, known by us as 'Hoddy' finally succeeded the other governesses. She was the best of them all and stayed until we went away to boarding school.

While Hoddy was in charge of us I had a very serious attack of measles which left me with a heart murmur. This was considered dangerous and I was made to go around in a wheelchair for a year. The first I had was a three-wheeler basket chair with a long metal bar attached to the front wheel which allowed me to steer in any direction I chose. On Hoddy's advice, it was replaced within the week by another without that option! I was not allowed to walk up and down stairs and, our nurseries being at the top of the house, this meant that our unfortunate governess had to carry me.

Soon after this all five of us, boys as well as girls, were sent to Glendower School in the Cromwell Road in South Kensington. I remember all of us being paraded in front of new parents by the Headmistress, to prove that Dr and Mrs Phillipps had enough faith in the school to send all their five children there at the same time! Later the boys went away to prep school and Stella and I went as boarders to West Heath in Sevenoaks. Christine, for some reason unknown to us, went to the Monkey Club in Pont Street and must have found it lonely in the house when she came home, with all her brothers and sisters away. I was not a particularly bright child, but I did not object to going away to school - apart from the compulsory games, which I detested. Whether my illness had turned me into a hypochondriac, or whether it had really damaged my heart, I am not sure, but I do remember that games lessons left me exhausted and blue round the lips.

It was at West Heath that I first experienced individual attention and the feeling that my opinion was worth expressing. As we advanced in age we were encouraged by the headmistress, Phyllis Elliott, to use our minds as well as our brains, and she put great value on original thought. She was responsible for enabling me to discover my love of the arts and for the growth of my imagination. She was an unusual woman who possessed a great gift for teaching and for leadership; her values became important to some of us and I owe her a great deal.

When I was seventeen my mother removed me from West Heath, although Stella stayed on. I think there were several reasons for my leaving, although they were not all explained to me. One may have been that my mother resented the important place which Phyllis Elliott held in my life. Perhaps she was jealous of Phyllis' influence over me, but more probably she was intimidated by Phyllis' intellectual ability. My mother definitely had feelings of academic inferiority which she revealed to me a long while later. She had never been to school, had always been taught at home, and had never had to sit an exam. I think she also had a feeling that too much learning could be dangerous!

Another reason for my leaving school was that my sister Christine was 'coming out' in the summer of 1938, and as neither my mother nor my father wanted to undertake the onerous job of chaperoning for longer than was necessary they had decided to bring out two daughters at once. I had no wish to 'come out' but I was removed from West Heath in the Spring of 1938 and thrown into the London Season.

Chapter 4

The London Season 1938

Before the Second World War the London Season ran to a standard form. 'Coming Out' was a respectable expression to use, and applied to many daughters of 'Society' families, particularly in London. Looking back, I see it as a shocking ritual, and I was vaguely aware of this even at the time. However, as it turned out, it was our last chance to enjoy our youth, and we did enjoy it. The Season began in May, and from then on until the end of July Chris and I, as *debutantes*, went to three or four dances plus several fork lunches and cocktail parties a week. There were the Ascot races, Henley Regatta and many other seasonal events which were great fun. We were able to buy new clothes, which had always been a rare event for me, as I had usually been expected to wear Chris's hand-me-downs. I frequented the 'Guinea Dress Shop' in Sloane Street and remodelled my four evening dresses between dances. *The Tatler* and *The Sketch* photographed the titled and the wealthy, and huge charity dances were given at the Dorchester and other hotels. On one of these occasions all the debutantes of the year (known as 'the Debs') had to wear white dresses and curtsey to a large, three-tiered cake, but what this somewhat heathen practice represented none of us ever discovered.

Later in the Season, when our parents had grown tired of it all, Chris and I were allowed out unchaperoned as long as we stayed together. However, we frequently broke this rule, separating from each other and going to night-clubs with our own individual friends, so that we came home at different times. There were many nights when I sat on the doorstep of No. 4 Lower Sloane Street waiting for a taxi to bring Chris home, so that we could go upstairs together without my mother realising that we had spent the evening in different places. She only allowed us to have one key, and that was always handed to us as we left the house and reclaimed on our return, in case we had copies made! How strange it is to think that at the age of seventeen I could doze on a doorstep in the middle of London at three o'clock in the morning and never have any feeling of worry that anything untoward might happen.

In June I fell in love. It was a new experience and it seemed as if a light had been turned on in my life and that the world was glowing with new meaning. Richard Magor was twenty-one and I thought him wonderfully good-looking: no dance was complete unless he was there. I was invited to his home, 'Springfield Lyons' in Chelmsford, for my first Hunt Ball and went down in trepidation. His parents were charming but I found them terrifying, while his sisters, all of whom were older than he was, treated him as if he were a school boy. This shook me, for I found him grown-up and glamorous. Soon after I arrived at the house, which was extremely large and rambling, Richard took me upstairs and introduced me to 'Nanny', who lived in a small room with her little dog. She obviously adored Richard. This visit to 'Nanny' was a ritual which was expected at the time, and many years later I was delighted to see a similar scene included in the film *Brideshead Revisited*.

When I unpacked my suitcase I found to my consternation that I had forgotten my evening shoes for the ball. It was Friday evening and the dance was on Saturday night. Pomeroy the butler became my good friend when I went to him to ask for his help. He was portly and kind and everything one could expect in a butler. He phoned my mother, who immediately put the shoes into the post. However, she had to wrap them individually because they would not fit into the letterbox wrapped together.

All through Saturday Pomeroy reported to me on the arrival of each post and, at last, one shoe turned up. By teatime I was in a panic, for one shoe was of little use, but with the four o'clock post came Pomeroy bearing a bedraggled parcel. The heel of the shoe had broken through the brown paper, a strap hung dejectedly outside the parcel, but the beaming butler presented it to me triumphantly on a silver salver as the family took tea in the drawing room. If I had not been so relieved I would have died of embarrassment, but the family (who, it seemed, had been informed of the crisis) rejoiced with me. The ice was broken and I began to feel more at home.

The summer was blissful. We danced and partied as if there was not a care in the world. One evening Richard kissed me on a bench in Berkeley Square and I had to tell him to stop when I saw a policeman coming. The policeman passed by with a polite "Good *evening*, sir" and we resumed our extremely tentative encounter. How strange that, more than sixty years on, I can still feel the warmth of the summer evening and hear the distant traffic, so unlike the roar of the present day, and see Richard's white tie shining in the light of the street lamps.

With the end of the Season came our final meeting: Richard was to be sent to Calcutta to the family business. When I went to lunch with him in the City for the last time he insisted that I drink a Pimm's No. 1 with him, which I did, although I was quite unaware that it was alcoholic until I had to negotiate the stairs after lunch. We parted on the platform of St Paul's Underground station, but there was little time for a farewell kiss. The train rushed in, the doors closed between us and I never saw him again. Recently I found a little carved jade dragon he sent to me through the post all the way from India. It had arrived miraculously undamaged in spite of being wafer-thin and enclosed in only an envelope. A few sad little letters passed between us but that was all.

Chris and I were presented at Court on the last occasion when such a ceremony took place. We had beautiful dresses, an ivory satin for Chris and a white lace lined with pink satin for me. Trains were an obligatory part of the presentation: Chris's was ivory satin and mine was pink and silver lame. My mother was being presented at the same time and all three of us wore the prescribed three curled white Prince of Wales ostrich feathers on our heads and carried a bouquet.

We were fetched from home in a Daimler, and sat in the Mall in a long queue feeling like goldfish in a bowl. People put their noses against the car windows, making comments such as, "Ooh, I like that one, the one in the pink dress," or "No, I think the other is better looking". They were completely unaware that the closed windows of the car did not exclude their conversation. My mother was intensely nervous but Chris and I thought it was a bit of a giggle. Our chauffeur drove slowly down the Mall in a queue of cars and eventually reached Buckingham Palace gates. On our arrival at the entrance, the car door was opened by a footman and we were escorted up a wide staircase into a waiting room. Some thoughtful person had arranged that we could also be directed to a cloakroom.

Standing in the anteroom on the threshold of the Throne Room, we waited for our names to be announced and the moment when we had to make our entrances. My mother was presented by a friend and she then presented Christine and me, which meant that our names were called out in turn as "Mrs Frederick Phillipps, presented by [the friend's name], presenting Miss Christine Phillipps and Miss Diana Phillipps." We made our court-curtsies to King George V1, backed out of the Throne Room, avoided tripping up on our trains, and passed on to line the long corridor down which the King would pass as he left the Throne Room.

A court-curtsey is more complicated than the brief bob which we now give when meeting Royalty. It takes quite a lot of practice and requires one to go right down to the floor while keeping the back straight and eyes on the King. Rising up again can look most ungainly unless well practised. The Queen was absent because her father had just died, and the King looked lonely and bored as we curtsied and paraded past him. I was sorry for him as I had no time for such things myself and felt that he must have thought it all a bit of a farce.

As we waited in line down the long corridor watching the King approaching after the ceremony, and preparing to make our final curtsey, my mother suddenly realised that her tulle veil, which was attached to the three ostrich feathers on her head, had become hooked up on the shoulder epaulette of the huge Beefeater who was standing to attention beside her. She realised that when she curtsied the feathers would be dragged off her head! Her agonised whispers directed me to get behind the Beefeater to untangle the veil, and luckily I managed to remove it just in time as the King appeared. My mother dropped a deep curtsey, but I could do nothing but crouch down behind the large, imposing back of the Beefeater, and pray that I would not be noticed.

At the end of June my sister and I had a Coming-Out dance at the Hyde Park Hotel. There were four hundred guests, a wonderful supper and band and, apart from drinks, it cost our father £1 a head! It was a great success, the huge ballroom decorated with pink flowers and the tables covered with pink linen cloths on which were vases of tiny pink roses.

The whole of that summer was quite wonderful. The weather was perfect and we skated at Streatham Ice Rink most weekends and learned to dance on ice with a group of boys who I remember with great affection, and who became our close friends. It was indeed a summer to end all the summers of our youth, but we were not to know that at the time. Many of the golden boys, none older than twenty-one, lived and loved so briefly, only to die in the war which broke out the following year.

Rumours of war had invaded our lives during 1938, and as 1939 crept closer we turned our minds to more serious matters. I worked with babies at the St. Thomas' Hospital Baby Centre, and frequently pushed six or more infants in an enormous wicker basket-pram between the Centre and St. Thomas's. The pram was hopelessly unwieldy and I had to ask for help every time I tried to negotiate a curb. Policemen held up the Embankment traffic for me and hoisted the load onto the far pavement, embarrassing me by their comments on how young I looked to have so many children, and other remarks in the same vein. The purpose of the journey, apart from the rather dubious one of giving the children some fresh air, was to collect their medicines from the hospital dispensary. I knew one or two of the young students studying at St Thomas' and always prayed that I would not meet them and have to endure their comments on my sudden maternity as well.

At this time I also passed a City and Guilds Examination in dressmaking and tailoring at the Chelsea Polytechnic, while Christine studied at an art school.

The artist James Gunn, known to us as 'Jimmy', was a great friend of my father and he generously allowed Chris to come to his studio for life drawing. My mother assumed that this would mean that Chris would be studying 'still life', but the truth, of course, was that the 'life' was a lot more mobile. Although she was very fond of Jimmy, my mother took a long time to get over the shock of entering his studio and finding Chris alone with him and a glamorous naked model! In the following years, Jimmy painted a portrait of my father and a small oil of my mother. He later became Sir James Gunn and was acknowledged as the greatest British portrait painter of his time.

Years later, long after he and my parents had died, I was reading *Good Housekeeping* in the hairdresser's one day and found myself looking at a small reproduction of one of Jimmy's paintings called *Gwen on the River Bank*. I recognised it immediately as a picture of my mother. In the painting she was wearing a very distinctive coat which I well remembered from my childhood. However, on reading the caption below the portrait, I discovered that it was thought to be a portrait of Jimmy's first wife, also named Gwen. I wrote to the gallery concerned and they put me in touch with Jimmy's daughter who, in turn, helped me to contact her brother, Paul. He had inherited their father's paintings. The brother and sister were both children of Jimmy's second wife, Pauline, but they agreed with me that the portrait was not of Gwen Gunn. I would have loved to own the painting myself but Paul was fond of it and certainly did not want to sell it, nor would I have been able to afford it. However, Paul later found the oil sketch which Jimmy had done of my father at the first sitting for his portrait, and I was able to buy this. It seems a better likeness of my father as I remember him, than the final large oil painting which my grandmother had commissioned. Of course the sketch is unfinished, but to me my father's expression is more fleeting and alive in it than in the finished portrait.

Chapter 5

The Summer of 1939 and the Outbreak of War

During the summer holidays of 1939 we went as usual to Hickling in Norfolk where my grandmother had her cottage. My mother and her sisters had spent much of their lives in Hickling when they were children, living at the Hall while their father worked in London. This year they and their families were distributed around various cottages and pubs in the village and many friends came to stay during the month of August. Unknown to us, it was the last time we were to see many of the boys who holidayed with us that year. September 3rd was only weeks away and was to change everyone's life and destroy thousands of our generation.

Anthony and Oscar Waterlow, for example, who spent much of the summer with us, were killed in the early part of the war, Anthony on *HMS Hood* and Oscar in a submarine lost somewhere in the Mediterranean. They were two of the most charming boys we knew and we looked upon them as brothers. Anthony was a convinced pacifist and had always been deeply distressed at the thought of violence. He held out at first against entering the forces but succumbed in the end and joined the Navy. A few weeks after he was posted he went down with the *Hood* when she was torpedoed in the North Atlantic off Iceland.

I was due to have my nineteenth birthday on the 28th August. My mother's sister Molly had arrived in England from South Africa for the summer and had come down to Norfolk with their other sister Clarice, so in all we were eleven children and five or six adults. The summer had been wonderful; we had sailed on the Broads, raced our twenty-two foot Norfolk gun punt and picnicked on the beach at Sea Palling. It seems now that we lived in a fool's paradise during the summer months, trying to believe that the threat of war had been averted.

Towards the middle of August I had a strange premonition that something of the greatest importance was about to happen to me. It was a personal certainty that someone was coming towards me from a great distance. Then one evening as I entered my grandmother's cottage, I saw a man standing across the room in the half-light of the oil lamps. His face was in darkness, for the cottage was old and the ceiling and the lamps were low, but I was immediately aware that somehow I had always known him. There was no need to speak and, at that moment, time stopped for both of us. I stood still in the darkened doorway and felt recognition stretch out between us. Later I found out that his name was Hugh Haswell.

The next morning we cycled together to Sea Palling. Hugh ran down the beach to the sea and swam out and along the shore, while I wandered up into the sandhills to be alone and watch him. I thought "This man has filled my heart. I am so filled with breath that I can no longer breathe. This fullness is physical and I can hold no more, but I am also so light that I could float above the earth. Where and when did I know him? Who is he? If I speak of it to him will I break the spell?"

He came up from the sea, found me in the sandhills and asked me if I was going to swim. I shook my head, and let the sand flow through my fingers. For the following two days we scarcely spoke at all, and yet we were acutely conscious of each other's presence. I later found out that he had experienced the same strange awareness that I had.

Norfolk 1939

Do you remember my darling
thin waves upon the stones,
the barren beach, the wind sighing?
Sea grass streaming on the sand-stung dunes
and gulls crying?
Numbed fingers fumbling mine
the sand flying?

I so aloof, yet longing,
you so brave, silence forsaking,
you spoke, and murmured,
"Are you going to bathe?"
the tension breaking.
While I, sifting a million grains of love
upon my lap, just shook my head.
And so it was my love,
and you are dead.

3rd September 1939

At eleven o'clock on Sunday morning we sat round my grandmother's table in the cottage and listened to the 'wireless'. The Prime Minister was speaking, telling us that we were at war. A stunned silence filled the room, broken by sobs from my grandmother. She had lost her eldest son in the previous war and her husband had died shortly afterwards. Like many of my generation, however, I felt that now at last we could act and make quick work of Germany's threat to the world. The time of waiting was over. There was a rising belief amongst young people in the justice of fighting against the evil we saw spreading across Europe, and we had yet to learn of suffering and loss.

There was a sense of foreboding throughout the country that the Germans would launch a huge air attack on Britain as soon as war was declared. So apprehensive were the air raid officials, that sirens sounded almost as soon as the Prime Minister had finished his announcement. One or two people had been supplied with whistles for such an emergency and blew them tentatively, but in general the village was ill-prepared for an alert.

Within a short time, however, the All Clear was sounded all over Britain, and people got down to fixing up their blackout curtains, pasting black paper over parts of the headlights of their cars, sticking strips of brown paper on the glass of their windows, and considering the state of their larders.

Leaving Nanny and the smaller children in the country, we returned to London. My Aunt Molly and her husband were in great haste to get home to South Africa before it became too dangerous to travel by sea. My mother's step-brother, Ned Crosse, searched for a passage to Singapore to join his brother Jack. Sadly, this set the seal upon the rest of his life, for Ned was to die of dysentery in the hospital of a Japanese prisoner of war camp. Night after night his brother Jack, who by then was confined in the same camp, crawled under the wire to be with him as he lay dying. Had Jack been caught, he would have been shot, but thankfully he at least returned home to England, although not for many years.

Arriving in London from Norfolk with the family, I remember sitting in the crowded taxi with Hugh, secretly holding hands. He was to return to Cambridge to join up with the RAF Volunteer Reserve. Parting from him, so soon after our first meeting, was devastating to me. His excitement at the thought of flying aeroplanes and rejoining his friends at the RAF Training School in Little Rissington, made it easier for him. I returned to 4 Lower Sloane Street, wrenched out of the dream which had carried me through the previous days. Doubt overwhelmed me, for there had been little opportunity in which to speak our thoughts. I began to wonder whether my imagination had fooled me and I suffered for twenty-four hours until his first letter arrived. It enabled me to place him securely, in his uniform, with his feet firmly on an aerodrome in another part of England, with me in his heart as he was in mine.

I was distracted to some extent from the chaos and apprehension which engulfed the whole country by the need to help my aunt Molly to pack for herself, her husband, and the three little girls, and particularly the many vital things which would be needed for the baby on the dangerous voyage back to Africa. The baby, Ian Gordon, was about nine months old and a precious son after three daughters. There was a real danger to shipping and Molly was instructed to pack emergency rations in case they had to take to the lifeboats. I recall her going out to buy a huge pair of navy blue knickers to pull on *over* her nightie in the event of an emergency! This was her only concession to Adolf Hitler. In fact she and her family travelled safely, for it turned out that the serious war was not to start at sea, or on the Home Front, for some months. I did not see her again for six years.

Hugh, who had previously been reading Law at Pembroke College, went with a number of his close friends to an RAF Flying Training School and was thrown immediately into an urgent course covering all aspects of wartime night-flying and navigation. He wrote enthusiastically and frequently and he phoned often. It was not easy for me to phone him as it was hard to locate him, but I was always aware when he was trying to get through to me. Later, when I was on a secretarial training course outside London, the phone was always in use and I would have to ask the others to ring off for a moment if I felt that he was trying to get through to me. Strangely, I was never wrong, and he always rang at just those moments. From these brief contacts after our first parting, I became aware of a telepathy between us, a gift which has never ceased throughout the following years.

Occasionally Hugh and his friends Claude Goldsmith and Tony Fry, who were all South Africans, would come to London on a weekend leave and we would cram ourselves into Claude's MG and go for a pub crawl. Sometimes, however, Hugh and I had an evening to ourselves, eating in small blacked-out restaurants in the Kings Road, or sitting on a bench in the cold autumn darkness of Hyde Park. My parents did not know about these meetings. They would not have been happy about us seeing each other, and things became harder and harder as the winter came on. Their objection to our friendship was because Hugh was a South African.

The problem was that my mother's sister Molly had gone to live in South Africa when she married a South African called Gordon Douglas. He had been befriended by my grandmother in 1918 when he came to England at the end of the war. She had met him as she served teas on Victoria Station to men returning from the Front, and so it was she who had introduced him to Molly. However, although Molly and her husband were very happy together, the marriage was looked on as a tragedy by the family in England, because it took Molly so far away.

(The trains bringing men home from France in 1918 had also brought prisoners from many different parts of the world, including a number of students who had been trapped in Germany in 1914. Amongst them was my mother's youngest brother, Aubrey, who had been a prisoner for four years. Aubrey's return was a great joy and helped my grandmother to get over the loss of her eldest son in 1916).

Because of my parents' feelings, Hugh and I had to resort to underhand means in order to get any time to ourselves. My mother always insisted on sitting in the drawing room with us if Hugh came to the house, and I was not permitted to take him up to my bed-sitting room. One way and another we made the best of our brief meetings and compensated with many letters for our months of enforced separation. Had we known what the future held we might have acted very differently. One of Hugh's letters contained the following poem:

O thou who hauntest me so oft in dreams,
From whose dear face my thoughts cannot escape,
Nor from that form and voice, or from the shape
Of scenes long past, of many hopeful schemes
That ruined fell as oft as they were made.

And yet I hope that in some time to come
Our love may triumph o'er the fearful shade
That, as a veil, is often cast by some,
And hides true thoughts, true love; so to evade
The revelation that one day must come.

Hugh Haswell

Chapter 6

MI5 and the Official Secrets Act

My secretarial training having finished, I came back to Lower Sloane Street in the spring of 1940. The bombing of London had not yet started. In May I joined MI5 as a personal secretary. My interview was very 'hole and corner' and I was not at all sure what sort of job I was getting into. My references were supplied by relatives in the Forces and I even had one from a well-known judge, the father of a friend of mine. I was instructed to turn up at an office in St. James' Street but to tell no one where I was going. Signing the Official Secrets Act was daunting: it gave me the feeling that at any moment I might make a terrible error and be arrested.

Shortly after my arrival the 'Office' moved to Wormwood Scrubs Prison. We were not permitted to tell anyone the name of the department or the place to which we had been moved. My Father was keen to find out what I was doing and tried all sorts of trick questions, such as "Have you met So-and-so?" and "What's it like to work for the Army?" The fact that we did not wear uniform might have led him to make a few guesses, but I got by without too much trouble. There were a few moments when I had to cover up quickly, but it was always safe to name the Ministry of Information if I was in a tight corner.

In those days I had a yellow bicycle, and on the first morning, after a long and complicated ride from Sloane Square to East Acton, I arrived at the intimidating gates of Wormwood Scrubs Prison. Showing my pass to the policeman at the prison gate, I was directed to the first enormous block of cells. Cat-calls and whistles followed me as I crossed the yard, for the cell block adjacent to the Office was still filled with prisoners. However, they were not to stay long, for they were soon evacuated to a 'place of safety,' while we, and the officers for whom we worked, remained to face whatever Hitler chose to throw against London.

'The Scrubs' was a terrifying place. Gates clanged behind me as I entered and, on the first day there, the woman in charge of female staff spent much time pasting newspapers on the walls of the lavatories in order that the 'gels' should not see what the prisoners had written, or the crude drawings they had left behind them. (We spent some time tearing the paper off again!) I was allotted a cell on the first floor, next door to the one occupied by Edward Cussen, for whom I was to work. He was a lawyer and I believe he became a judge after the war. He had also only just arrived, so we both sat in our cells waiting for something to happen, with no idea how we were to begin working. I was dependent on work given to me by him and he had not yet discovered what he was meant to be doing. However we did at least have the opportunity to get to know each other.

I soon discovered that once you had entered your cell and closed the door it was not possible to open it again. In an emergency you had to phone up your officer to come and let you out, but at first we had no telephones so urgent shouts could be heard at intervals from along the walkways which circled the interior of the building. Wire netting had been slung between the balconies to prevent suicides amongst the prisoners. Another disconcerting discovery was that each door had a peephole through which you could be observed. If you wanted to adjust your stockings, or something like that, the only safe position was to stand close to the left or right hand wall on either side of the door. I was lucky in having a particular friend in the Office called Billie, who had been there for a few months. Through her I was able to discover how the Office was managed, but she was, of course, also new to Wormwood Scrubs and no one made much headway for a few weeks.

A personal secretary was looked upon as being in an exalted position by the many girls who worked for MI5, especially those who were known as 'snaggers'. The snaggers, poor things, had to spend their lives hunting for lost files, which were either wrongly marked out to various people or were being 'sat on' by officers for different reasons.

Snaggers worked from the Registry, which was housed in a large tin hut along one side of the prison block. The Registry was the heart of the Office and many of the other girls who worked there had very interesting jobs. Within the hut was held the card index and all the records and files, without which the Office could not have existed. It seems strange in retrospect that such an important aspect of MI5 should have been housed in such a vulnerable position in a tin-roofed shed.

Later that summer I was told to take over the position of personal secretary to Roger Hollis, the head of Section F. I knew that he had a reputation for being difficult and exacting and I was terrified. My hand shook so much when I was taking shorthand from him that I could scarcely read it back. I don't suppose that he was really as bad as I thought, but I was very young and in my first job.

I had arrived in MI5 at an eventful time. The tragic miracle of Dunkirk had just happened and Britain was in turmoil. Winston Churchill had just become Prime Minister and had sacked Major-General Sir Vernon Kell, the man who had been in charge of the Office since 1909. Brigadier Harker filled in for a time, but was soon replaced by Sir David Petrie. Unknown to the Office as a whole, much was happening at that period of the war. We heard the occasional rumour of spies being caught and sabotage taking place but secrecy was paramount in MI5 and the left hand, very sensibly, did not not know what the right hand was doing.

At this critical moment my own life suffered a shattering blow, which meant that I had to combine taking on my new job with trying to overcome personal grief.

In June 1940 I had been down to see Hugh at Andover where he was completing his Flying Training Course, particularly concentrating on night flying. We had planned one whole glorious summer day in the country together and, by careful calculation, I managed to miss the last train back to London. My phone call to my parents caused chaos; family friends were found in the area for me to stay with in order to keep my reputation intact. My mother seemed to believe that 'bad things' only happened at night: it never seemed to have occurred to her that they might happen in the country in the day-time!

In spite of family protests, Hugh and I spent the next day, Sunday, together. Then he returned to his RAF station and I, sadly, boarded a train back to London. Later he was posted to RAF Thorney Island to fly Blenheim bombers. He was, as so many of the young pilots were, intent on flying Spitfires or large bombers, but he was too large to fit into a Spitfire and, much to his annoyance, he was sent to a squadron of Blenheim bombers which flew reconnaissance flights across the English Channel and along the coast of France. I thought that he would be safer there than elsewhere, but night after night, during the few weeks he was there in the summer of 1940, I worried about him, and blessed the weather if it was unsuitable for operations to take place.

I had managed to see him one more time for a weekend in London before he went to Thorney Island. Hyde Park had been our rendezvous for most of that weekend. The July weather was wonderful and we made the best of it. We could not go to my home because of the serious row I had had with my parents, over the previous meeting we had managed to achieve in Andover. Our closeness had developed in a way which can only happen in the tension of war and in the face of the fear of death. We had little need to talk, for we were aware of each other at a depth which did not require words. Our time was like Dante Gabriel Rossetti's

> ....*close-companioned inarticulate hour*
> *When two-fold silence was the song of love.*

On that Sunday evening, after a day of closeness which I shall never forget, we parted at the north gate of Hyde Park. Hugh walked on to Paddington Station after putting me into a taxi to return home, for he could not face leaving me alone on the station platform as his train pulled out. I wept in the taxi, and was comforted by the kindness of the driver who pushed back the partition and tried his best to cheer me up.

On the night of Thursday 25th July, 1940, I had a dream. In the dream I was getting married to Hugh in a great London church, and I was walking up the aisle with my father. As we drew near to the altar the dream turned into a nightmare, for the man awaiting our arrival turned towards us and I realised that it was not Hugh. I fled from the church, tearing across what seemed to be the Norfolk marshes, pursued by police cars with sirens blaring. I woke in terror, convinced that Hugh was dead and that he had given me the dream as a warning.

The following morning I went to the office and told Billie that I knew Hugh had been killed, but she said she was sure that I would have heard if it had been so. Nothing would convince me that he had not died, but I had no means of finding out whether this was so. Two days later Hugh's sister rang our house early in the morning and told my mother that she had found a telegram in her post box saying that Hugh had been reported 'Missing'. I had heard the phone ringing in my mother's bedroom on the floor below mine and had known immediately what it meant - so much so that when my mother called up the stairs to me, I told her not to tell me because I already knew. She said 'He is not dead, darling, only missing', but I told her that I knew he had died. Later I was to find out that he had disappeared on the evening of the night on which I had been given the dream.

Hugh had undergone intensive RAF training during the months before joining his Squadron which was stationed in West Sussex on Thorney Island on the coast. He had a gift for writing, and even in the midst of his training, he had written poetry in his letters to me. Looking back from sixty years on I can see how young I was at nineteen compared to his twenty-one years. The upbringing I had had with my family in London had not prepared me for the desolation I was now experiencing. Because Hugh and I had recognised each other at the first moment of our meeting, and knew then that we had always known each other, we had not wasted a moment of the eleven months we were permitted in this life, even though we had so few days together. My deep and lasting regret was my failure to have his child.

The possibility of his dying had never been discussed between us. I suppose he did not talk about it because he did not want to alarm me, while I was afraid that putting my fear into words would undermine his courage. In retrospect, I do not think that those who fought in the Battle of Britain had time to consider what the future held for them. Death still seemed a distant prospect even when close friends began to disappear. Hugh was one of the first to die in the Battle of Britain, having been reasonably safe until he joined his Squadron at the beginning of July. No-one could have guessed that three weeks later he would have flown out of this life into the unknown.

How can one write about love, when there are no words with which to express the joy and pain, the longing and the loss? I learned then that there is no end to the pain of loving and that, however short the time given, the power of love does not diminish, for love lies in the realms of eternity and is not in this dimension.

As the months went by I stood alone on the edge of chaos. That Hugh was officially 'Missing' took from me the one way out by suicide, for, although I knew in my heart that he would not return, I was constantly encouraged to keep hoping. There was an aspect of myself which denied the inner knowledge of his death, a human need to hope against hope, ignoring the deeper certainty that he had gone beyond recall. My reaction to his dying precluded the help which I now know he was holding out to me. My life became a cycle of running from reality and returning to the agony of truth. I cannot explain the turmoil into which I had fallen. I knew of no place on this earth where I might find the body I loved, for Hugh had gone in reality "as a dream dies at the opening day," The manner of his dying was unknown to me, or to anyone else, both at that time and over the following years.

A funeral may seem harrowing but the placing of a body in a grave, or into the fire, allows one to accept the fact that the body, at least, no longer exists. With no body, no funeral and no final ceremony it was hard to accept the bitter truth of his death. The ceremony of marriage had also been denied to us, for my parents' attitude had made it impossible even to announce our engagement. We had in fact decided to get married once I had passed my twentieth birthday, but that date was a month away from the day of his dying.

Sixty years later, as I write this account, Hugh has never been declared anything but 'Missing'. His name appears on the RAF memorial to the 20,000 airmen who died and 'who have no known graves'. I have lived the rest of my life as if for two people - two people with one soul to hold them both - and the sense of oneness has never diminished. Beneath the surface lies the impossible, the strange, sudden realisation that two people on this earth can become one and live on in another dimension. There have been strange events over the years, which I will write about later, but for the moment I must return to 1940 and the war.

The Silver Tree

I slept at night in a single bed
in a house that was tall and grey,
soft sounds of the city in snow and sleet
as gas lamps burned in the empty street
and all night long shed a wanton glow
to the pools of light on the road below,
awaiting the coming day.

And high in the house of the climbing stairs
I nursed my hope in a lonely bed,
dreams drifting in through the shrouded dawn
circled and settled about my head,
and I was a bird awake to the sky
as the sun rose over my sleeping form,
and I soared and stooped in the misted air
to a place of trees in their pale spring leaves,
and many a tree held out to me
with branches stretched for a place to rest,
but I passed them by with a soft bird cry
and swiftly flew on my dreaming quest.

As evening came...

As evening came, and a call to sleep
was strong in the heart and the failing wing,
I circled down to a silver tree
which grew alone on a holy hill;
its leaves were whispering words to me
and teaching my dreaming heart to sing.
So all night long he sang his song,
a murmuring lilting lullaby,
for I was captive closed in arms
dark branches etched on a misted sky.
That night, that day, and day and night
we sang the summertime away,
my tree my refuge my delight.

But ever in the creeping dawn
when curtains drew the daylight in,
I rose and searched in vain to see
my loving, gentle singing tree.
Beyond the roofs and city gloom
my heart was trapped within.

Then autumn with its harvest moon
brought back my dream and I was free,
with coppered wings and feathered flight
I left the city house and home
and soared with joy into the night.
So long I searched the dream grew pale
I clasped it close nor let it die,
yet ever on across the world
beneath a torn and ragged sky,
I journeyed to that holy place
where warmth and love were found.

At morning when the night was gone,
the dream fast fading in the light,
I found the barren ground.
No silver tree of love was there,
a hollow grave upon the hill
marked where his youthful roots had grown,
when men with axe and ropes had come
his singing life to kill.

I had no power with which to fly,
no love to lift me from that place.
I know not where his branches lie
nor whether trees retain their grace
in fields of green and pastures new.
Yet in this life my eyes still see
my living, branching, silver tree.

Chapter 7

The London Blitz

The London Blitz, at the beginning of September 1940, seemed like the culmination of all suffering. There was a universal fear which united people, making the pain of the individual one with the pain of all. I prayed that my life might end with a bang and not a whimper, that a bomb might achieve for me that which I had not had the courage to do for myself.

Every morning and evening I rode my banana-coloured bike from Sloane Square to work at MI5 in Wormwood Scrubs Prison. At first, in the summer months, before the war came close to London, it was quite a pleasant ride from Chelsea to East Acton, but gradually it became more and more difficult. Sirens began to alert us to dog-fights over the city and it was then necessary to go down into one of the many shelters along the route. At the beginning of September, when the real Blitz began, the Docklands were targeted night after night and the air-raid warnings seemed continuous. Each morning, after disturbed nights, sleeping on a camp-bed in my siren suit in the basement of No 4 Lower Sloane Street, I dragged my bike up the stone steps of the 'area', where the coal was kept below the house, and started out for the Office. Every day the roads were blocked with fallen houses or unexploded bombs and I had to find another way through. As I returned, the evenings darkened and the sky glowed red with horrific fires in the East End. Fire-engines roared to the docks and the fire and ambulance services were stretched to the limit. My journeys home became more and more complicated.

One evening I was returning with a very tiny spaniel puppy in my bicycle basket. It belonged to someone else who, for some reason, could not take it home with them. I thought nothing of it until I was ordered into a shelter as sirens shrieked and bombers drummed overhead. Then I discovered that I was not permitted to take a dog into the shelter. The puppy was only about six weeks old, so I could not possibly leave it with the bike in the street. I rushed on, hoping not to be stopped again, but a few streets further on the same thing happened. However, as there was no law forcing one to enter a shelter I finally managed to run the gauntlet and reach home.

I had always believed that the instinctive fear which leads us to duck when a blow comes, or to go down to the depths of the cellar when air-raids start, would be overcome by losing the will to live. This was proved otherwise to me on a night in the autumn of 1940.

At the height of an intense air raid on Chelsea, I was alerted to the fact that our tall London house had fire-bombs on the roof, and I found myself tearing up the stairs to get to them. My parents were out, manning the Chelsea Mobile Unit (a wartime medical emergency response unit), and there was no-one available to help me apart from a friend of my father's, Maurice, who was staying the night. I gathered up the stirrup-pump from the attic and, leaving Maurice in the attic below, carried the hose onto the roof while he pumped water out of a tin bath which we kept filled in case of just such an emergency.

Knowing that it was important to direct a spray and not a jet onto phosphorous bombs, I had to make a guess in the dark as to which way to push the switch on the hose. I made the wrong guess and the three bombs exploded and spread the fire in front me. The feeble jets of water issuing from the nozzle of my little stirrup pump disappeared in steam without appearing to affect the heat of the three bombs, which burned in a twisted heap on the lead roof. I do not know how long we pumped and sprayed our inadequate jets of water in the direction of the fire, but it seemed an age. The lead roof must have been fairly thick for the bombs did not fall through into the rooms below.

Standing high above London, I had a sense of exultation as the fires burned all around. Fire-engines clanged their way through the debris of Lower Sloane Street below me, ambulances howled, and guns opened up on the small silver bird-like shape of a plane, caught in the crossbeams of the searchlights. I stood entranced for a brief moment, as if the fires of hell were rising through the city and the last days had come. I could feel no anger against the perpetrators of the chaos, one of whom was up there flying above me in a terrifying hail of shells and tracer bullets. There, over another country, had things been different, might have been Hugh. I remember praying that the plane would get away, that the young man within it would live. Then, with the suddenness of waking from a dream, I heard the whistle of the first steel shards of shrapnel falling from the exploding shells and embedding themselves in the lead roof around me.

The instinct for self-preservation overtook me. I catapulted down through the skylight, missed the ladder and fell onto Maurice, who was still frantically pumping water from the bath in the attic below. As I fell my body became ensnared in the rope which controlled the enormous sky-light, which then crashed down, showering us with glass. Poor Maurice must have thought we had been hit by a bomb. We extricated ourselves from the debris, climbed out of the bath and ran down the stairs in panic. Only when we reached the basement did we stop to discover whether we had come to any harm, but, apart from a cut on my thumb, we had received no more than shock.

Shortly afterwards my mother, who was with my father at the Unit in Tite Street Hospital, rang up to tell me not to panic, but that one of the houses in Lower Sloane Street was on fire. I told her that we had three phosphorous bombs on the roof, but added that I hoped that I had managed to put them out. She could not come back as she was on duty as a nurse with the Unit which was likely to be called out at any moment because bombs were falling in the Chelsea district. I must have caused her serious worry.

My father and mother were with the Chelsea Mobile Unit throughout the war. This meant that they had to report to their headquarters whenever there was an air raid which looked like involving our part of London, and had to be ready to attend every bomb incident which happened in Chelsea during their time on duty. I was usually left in the house sleeping in the basement with the parlour-maid and the dog. The dog was a great responsibility, as he was terrified of loud noises, and at night I had to tie his lead to my foot in case he ran from the house in an emergency. In the end we had to evacuate him to the country.

My father was extremely brave during the Blitz. Apart from many smaller incidents, two particularly bad ones involved the Unit. One was the bombing of the Sloane Square Underground station. A train was moving out of the station as the bomb exploded, blocking the escape of those who were in the front of the train and killing most of those in the rear. The front passengers had to walk along the line to South Kensington Station before they could be rescued. My father took over the Royal Court Hotel as a casualty clearing station and commandeered a house in Eaton Square as a mortuary. The injuries were appalling and late that night, by the aid of a torch, he had to go through the mortuary to make sure that he had not made any errors. He was worried that in the confusion someone still living might have been brought there in error. This was a gruesome business and he came home shattered.

An incident which was even worse for him happened beneath the World's End block of flats in the Kings Road. The heavy rescue squad had tunnelled down to where a little boy lay with his legs trapped under a concrete beam. He was alive but his mother and sister were dead beside him. My father was a large man and it was not easy for him to reach the child by way of the tunnel, which was in any case dangerous and liable to collapse, but somehow he managed to reach the place where the child lay. The building was on fire above and firemen were trying to control the fire to keep it away from the rescuers. However, the water from their hoses was collecting in the basement where the child was and threatening to drown him and his rescuers.

A young RAF man on leave was down another tunnel trying to calm the child. The only possibility was to amputate both the boy's legs in order to get him out, but this would have needed an open anaesthetic, which would have been impossible because of the fire. In order to perform an amputation, my father would have had to operate hanging head first down under the burning house, without proper instruments. Anaesthetics by injection were not available as they are now and my father became certain that the child would die from pain, shock and loss of blood, and that there would be no way to save him before the fire reached them. In the end my father had no alternative but to give the boy a large dose of morphia and stay as long as it was necessary to know that the drug had worked, before leaving him with his mother and sister. Just in time, Dad was pulled backwards out of the tunnel by the rescue squad. Later he was awarded the MBE for the part he had played, a strange award for risking your life, but at least his bravery was recognised.

In November 1940 a 500-pound bomb exploded in the basement of our house in Lower Sloane Street, blowing up the gas mains, the water supply and the drains and damaging the fabric of the building, so that it was no longer habitable. Freda, the parlour maid, was there alone that night and was taken to hospital with shock and blast damage to her lungs. However, she recovered and returned to help my mother and father when they moved to a flat in Lowndes Square, where they were to remain for the rest of the war.

Siren Sounds and Phosphorus Bombs

Oh do not write
of the tropical seas
from the stern of a ship
when celestial dark
reveals in the night
unbelievable light
of the phosphorus glow
in the wake of the ship
on the surface of sea
but turn back the page
to the sound of the sirens
that sing out the fear
of the roar in the darkness
as bombers appear
to scatter their gifts
wrapped in silver
and whistling screams
in a fire-bearing
torrent of danger
as life-killing streams
on the cities below
in the blackout
and noise of the guns
and the bells
as the fire engines rush
to the horror of hells
which were homes

I stand on the roof
in the presence of death
and breathe in the breath
of the phosphorus fumes
facing the prospect
of life after death
the hose in my hand
sends a pitiful stream
which leaps from the flames
in a column of steam
and guns in the street
track invaders in flight
while shards from their shells
fall like spears in the night

so swiftly retreating
I fall through the door
in panic descending
down floor after floor
alone in the basement
deep under the stair
alive in my mind
is the phosphorus glare
as it melts through the lead
in a visualised glow
and burns through the rafters
and ceilings below

but down in the cellar
my terrors retreat
I climb to the roof
where the phosphorus heat
has scorched through the ceiling
its thrust ending there

only smudges of smoke
linger on in the air,
no signs of the fire
which I dreaded appear,
just stench of scorched wood
where I fell in my fear,

and sirens are calling
to sound the All Clear.

September, 1940

Chapter 8

MI5 1940 to 1943

The beautiful summer of 1940 passed by, but at MI5 we worked seven days a week and had no time for relaxation. I was still secretary to Roger Hollis and was gradually getting used to his way of working. He was a cynical, monosyllabic man who never let the slightest slip pass him by. I began to wonder whether he was ill, for he was certainly worried and overtired.

There was an occasion when a man in a flat below ours in Lowndes Square was arrested. I was asked by my mother if I thought he was a spy, and had to keep a blank look on my face because in fact I knew quite a lot about him. My mother told me that a post office engineer who had come to mend her telephone had told her he had been employed to 'tap' the telephone of the man in the flat below. I was horrified to hear this, as such things were supposed to be strictly secret. Some time later, she told me that a man had come to see her about the incident and that she was afraid that "the nice engineer" was going to get into trouble. I must have shown by my expression that I was somehow involved, because she was sure that it was I who had passed on the information. That the engineer concerned was a threat to the security of the country never seemed to enter her mind. Interestingly, it turned out that the man who had come to interview my mother was my boss Roger Hollis.

One morning in November 1940, at a time when the raids on London were severe, I cycled to the Scrubs as usual to find firemen and hoses all over the prison yard. A bomb had fallen on the Registry during the night. This was a disaster for the Office and for the defence of the country. It was, however, looked on as a 'lark' by many of the girls who worked in that department, as they all had to go home. Because my part of the Office was within the prison block, we were able to remain at work, but it soon became apparent that there was no way in which MI5 could continue to work without access to the Registry.

Roger Hollis was deeply worried, and angry that so many of the staff did not realise what a catastrophe the bomb had caused. He told me something which I doubt whether many people knew at the time, or have indeed realised since. Apparently he had been instrumental in having MI5's entire card-index photographed and sent to Canada a short while before the bomb fell. The photographs had only just reached their destination and had to be shipped straight back to London. Many years later, when Hollis was suspected of being the Fifth Man in the spy ring which had infiltrated MI5 and MI6, I wondered how knowledge of this particular episode might have affected those who were judging him. I was always certain that Roger was not implicated in the spy ring; I did not think that his character was that of a spy. However, when eventually the whole story came out, it was obvious that even those who worked closely with Philby, the prime member of the spy ring, had no idea where *his* loyalties lay, so I could have been mistaken.

As it turned out, when the photostats of the card-index returned from Canada after the bomb incident, they were almost indecipherable. The machine used to photograph them had blurred each one by passing them through too quickly. In those days the machine was operated by hand, and as I write this on my computer at the beginning of another century the information technology of that time seems to have all been incredibly primitive.

An enormous amount of time was wasted in the Office as we did our best to overwrite every one of the thousands of cards which comprised the index. The files, and some cards which had been in steel cabinets, were burned all round the edges leaving only the centres readable. These were the files in use for the next few years and the smell of wet, burnt paper emanating from them was terrible. We ended each day with filthy hands and carried the smell of charred paper in our hair and on our clothes when we went home at night.

The Office was moved as soon as possible to Blenheim Palace in

Oxfordshire. This might have seemed a beneficial move for the workers in the Registry, but as secretaries we missed our little individual cells, for it was freezing in the tin huts in the yard of the Palace. The Registry workers were much more comfortable, having left their tin shed for the interior of the Palace and a fairly warm existence. Fleets of cars and buses took us from London to Woodstock and we were found digs in houses around the area. Eventually Keble College in Oxford was requisitioned for female staff and about three hundred of us were housed there. On a cold, grey winter night a friend and I were shown to our room in the college by an elderly 'scout' who greeted us with the cheerful news that "The last man what 'ad this room 'anged 'imself, Miss." I was not surprised.

There were six bathrooms in an ice-cold clock-tower across the quad and more than three hundred women to share them. (It seemed that as students were usually only in residence for two or three months at a time, washing facilities came low on the list of priorities). We slept two to a unit originally designed for one person. Each unit had a small sitting-room with a single bed and a tiny fireplace, but practically no coal. A minute bedroom was screened off from the sitting room with room for another small bed, and there were lavatories, a communal kitchen and a laundry down a long passage.

Men could visit us, but had to be out by eleven o'clock at night. However, as many of the women were married this rule frequently went unobserved. If the man in question had not left by eleven the only option was for him to climb out over the wall, or stay all night and leave at a respectable time in the morning. It also occasionally happened that old Keble students, on leave with nowhere to go, would climb into Keble to doss down for the night, unaware that it had suffered a wartime change. They must have had mixed feelings when they encountered women in flimsy nighties flitting about the ill-lit corridors.

The buses arrived every morning at seven o'clock to ferry us from Keble to Blenheim, where we could get breakfast at the canteen. There was really very little secrecy as to our destination. At Blenheim Palace we showed our pink identity cards to the police at the gate and were admitted to the Palace Yard. It was not unknown for those who had forgotten their passes to show the corner of a pink cheque book instead!

Hugh Astor (who had become Hollis' PA) and I tried to keep a light-hearted atmosphere at work, and in this we were helped by Roger Fulford, the historian, who was also part of the other half of our Section. He was a delightful man and a great asset to have around.

Part of my work required that I should go up to a small room in the comparative seclusion of the gate-tower. I never found out how it happened, but one day the tower was discovered to be in flames and the local fire-engine arrived. Many wax cylinders were stored in the tower for use in our work and they must have burned fiercely. No-one was suspected of sabotage, but this was the second time that the fire service had had to deal with those parts of the Office which were meant to be kept under strict security.

My work for Roger Hollis was not easy, for he was not a friendly man. I dare say that he was under stresses of which I knew nothing, for things were not going smoothly at that time of the war and he was in a very responsible position. I remember that one day, when our office had been moved inside the Palace, Winston Churchill suddenly entered the Section accompanied by numerous members of his family. (The Duke and Duchess of Marlborough, who were normally resident in the other parts of Blenheim Palace, were of course his close relatives). Churchill's visit put Roger in a dilemma, as no one was permitted in our offices without a valid reason and without having signed the Official Secrets Act. Casual visitors would never have been admitted under any circumstances. Roger leaned across his desk and, very obviously, turned all the files face downwards. Churchill, on the far side of the desk, took the hint and sent his relatives out! He then sat down and showed enormous skill as he questioned Roger on various aspects of his work. Trapped in the corner of the room behind the desk - having been taking shorthand when they arrived - I was most impressed at the knowledge shown by Churchill, who was able to discuss confidential matters in detail with Hollis.

(Anyone interested in this period of the war is recommended to read Nigel West's book *MI5 British Security Service Operations 1909-1945*.)

Chapter 9

Oxford and Marriage

Late in 1942, when MI5 had been in Oxford for two years, I was introduced by a friend called Anthony Batty-Shaw to the men who were doing fire-watching at Rhodes House in Oxford. Most of them had come to England from overseas on Rhodes Scholarships (scholarships bequeathed to many students by Cecil Rhodes) and were delighted to take on the fire-watching in return for free and comfortable digs. It was a great joy for me to spend some time there instead of in the gloom of Keble College.

I was not in the habit of going out much at this period of the war, having become used to leading a reclusive life after Hugh's death. However the Rhodes House group were a cheerful lot and by 1942 a number of the girls from Keble College had struck up friendships with them. I am afraid we seriously interrupted their medical studies. They all slept in a dormitory at the top of the house so as to be available if an emergency should occur, although in fact bombers avoided Oxford throughout the war.

The Rhodes Scholars had access to a well-equipped kitchen at Rhodes House and had become quite good cooks. As far as I can remember their menus were more or less limited to roast birds which they acquired from landowners with shoots round and about, but dinners there were always a great treat after the MI5 canteen and the depressing little meals we managed to cook up in the communal kitchens in Keble.

I became very friendly with several of the men who lived in Rhodes House and with their friends and girlfriends. Some of the Rhodes Scholars were medical students at the Radcliffe Infirmary, and amongst them was a young man called Robert Fynn. He was a Rhodesian, the youngest son of Sir Percy and Lady Fynn who lived in Salisbury, the capital city of what was then Southern Rhodesia. For many years Sir Percy had been the Minister of Finance in the Rhodesian Government under Sir Godfrey Huggins (later Lord Malvern).

In the autumn of that year at one of the Rhodes House dances, Robert Fynn asked me to marry him. I was amazed, having had no idea that such a possibility was even in the offing. Even more amazingly, the same evening another man, also a medical student, put the same question to me. I had to admit to him that I had already had a similar offer! I did not accept Robert immediately and he went off to spend Christmas in Scotland while I had time to consider the question. (I had a feeling that he had gone up there to discover if another girl, whom he knew in Scotland, would suit him better! Whether this was so or not I never discovered). However, when he returned he still seemed to think that my answer would be a foregone conclusion.

By 1943 I had reluctantly accepted Hugh's death. I had known beyond all doubt for several years that he would never return. Only some years later did I realise that the gift of psychic knowledge, which had existed so strongly between us, was to continue indefinitely.

For some reason my parents, who had been so much against my engagement to Hugh because he was a South African, did not raise any objection to my engagement to Robert Fynn, a Rhodesian, but this may have been because neither they nor I considered the possibility that he would ever go back to live in Rhodesia. My father offered him a partnership in his medical practice, and Robert was very keen to take up the offer. In the end when I agreed to marry him it seemed certain that we would be living in London, close to my family.

We were married four months after we met, because Robert was likely to be called up and sent overseas when he qualified. Looking back, I am amazed that I agreed to marry him so soon after our first meeting. It turned out that his brother Ted, who was a great charmer, told Robert that if he (Robert) did not marry me, then he (Ted) would, and this spurred Robert on to push for an early date. I only learned this from Ted many years later.

All my really close friends had been killed in the first years of the war and life was lonely. Only those who have been through the day-to-day suffering of such a time and have become used to seeing no future ahead, can understand that wartime decisions were very often made under pressure and without clear thought.

Chaos and tension mounted in the family as my mother tried to arrange our wedding in London while I was in Oxford. I did not want a big white wedding and would have much preferred a quiet family one, but Robert and my mother wanted the whole works. Because of the difficulty of having very few clothing coupons I planned to wear my grandmother's wedding dress, which was very beautiful. Her waist had been very small when she had worn it, and although my waist was not large adjustments had to be made. It was altered by adding a length of Brussells lace from my grandmother's collection. The lace was in one piece, handmade, very valuable and yards long, and it was added to the width of the skirt and the bodice by being carried up the left front of the dress, round the neck as a stand-up Elizabethan collar, down the right front and round the hem, the rest of the long length somehow being concealed underneath the train. I also wore my mother's veil. My grandmother supplied her clothing coupons to enable Robert to have a winter overcoat and some much needed underwear, and I managed to get seven days' leave from MI5.

The night before the wedding my mother came into my bedroom and said rather tentatively, "Darling, you do know how cats have kittens, don't you?"and went on to say, "Do remember, darling, doctors are only men..." She had also married a doctor, and may have been thinking of her own wedding night. We did not continue this conversation because I could see her embarrassment; she found it very difficult to talk about sex.

On the day of the wedding, when everyone had gone to the church and only my father and I remained in the flat, I was overcome with panic and told him that I could not go through with it. My sense of fear and foreboding was very real but it had come too late. My poor father was at a loss and said, "My dear old girl, you can't do this to me! Have a whisky." I realised that he was right - I could not do it to him - and, assisted by the strength of a small and unaccustomed tot, I overcame my intuition and went forward into the rest of my life.

We left for Holy Trinity, Brompton, in a Daimler and as I entered the Church I found myself in the midst of the dream which had been given to me the night Hugh was killed. I was now in reality in the huge church of my dream, walking up the aisle on my father's arm with friends in the pews around me, and Robert waiting near the altar. At that moment sirens wailed to warn of an air-raid. It was, I think, the sound of the air-raid sirens screaming - as the police-car sirens had in the dream - which convinced me that the original dream had been precognitive. This time I did not run from the church. By then I had realised that the message given to me by Hugh at the time of his death was that I would be married, but that it could not be to him. I was so shaken by the replay of my dream that I remember little of the service.

The reception after the wedding was a small one in my parents' flat in Lowndes Square but afterwards, thanks to my dear Uncle Aubrey, we had a party at the Hungaria Restaurant. The Hungaria was chosen partly because it had an underground reception room which could offer some safety in an air raid, and partly because Vecchi, the owner of the restaurant, was a great friend of my uncle. At the time we did not know it, but Aubrey had helped Vecchi to get Jewish musicians out of Hungary as the Germans advanced across Europe, and Vecchi was deeply grateful to him.

What followed after the wedding-party was a trauma which sadly affected me in the future, and in the following paragraphs I have tried to be fair in my description of it.

I should perhaps explain that my parents' disapproval of my meeting with Hugh, and Hugh's own concern for me, meant that we never consummated our love before his tragic death. He was very aware that his life would be in danger in the Air Force, and his first thought was for me if I had been left with a child (and in those days an illegitimate child was shameful in a way which can hardly be imagined nowadays).

However, my love for Hugh, a gentle and deeply understanding person, had left me with a vision of what it could be like to find someone who, like me, would want to put love first in a marriage, and it was with these memories in mind that I approached my marriage to Robert. The fact that he was in a caring profession gave me hope for our future together.

After the reception we arrived at Brown's Hotel on a cold winter night in the London blackout. The first mistake I made was to sign my maiden name in the register and therefore I had to change it, which annoyed Robert. He had not booked a room with a bathroom attached and we were taken to a room with two single beds and a communal bathroom down a long passage. The blackout arrangements shed a cold blue light on the whole place and there was no hot water in the bedrooms or the bathrooms. None of this could be helped in wartime, when air raids were frequent and the blackout was strict, but it was not an attractive scene for a honeymoon.

I think I had been brought up to believe that marriage would be wonderful, mainly because my parents had never ceased to be in love. However it soon became apparent that Robert was not on my wavelength at all. Shivering with apprehension and cold, I undressed and put on a glamorous nightdress made for me by my grandmother, while Robert appeared in a decrepit pair of old Airtex pants which hung in shreds from the waistband. (I had seen them in his laundry months before, and had begged him to throw them away, but he had obviously kept them, despite being given clothing coupons by my grandmother to buy new underwear. He eventually threw the old pants into the wastepaper basket of our hotel room. Being rather strictly brought up I was shocked to imagine what the maid would think in the morning!)

Things did not go as I had pictured them. There was no opportunity for love-making as I had imagined it - in fact, I do not remember that the word 'love' was even mentioned. It seemed to me that if Robert had thought of the word at all, it meant only one thing to him. I was left in a state of pain and shock with all my dreams shattered. Later in the night as Robert slept in the bed on the far side of the room, I sat on the edge of the other bed and tried to consider the situation through my tears. It seemed that I had two options, to stay or to leave, but neither option was going to be easy. In both cases the quality of my life seemed to have been drastically altered. The outlook was bleak if I stayed and it would be a disaster if I left and tried to return to my parents. I had nowhere else to go. I was married to Robert, and by the end of the night I realised that I really had no choice at all.

Robert and I never discussed the matter in the years that followed, which was, I am sure, a mistake. I never discovered whether he had any idea of the harm he had done to me, and he seemed unaware that there were any lasting problems. During the night I had packed my case in preparation for leaving and was dressed in my travelling clothes when he woke in the morning. I had not slept at all. I was in considerable pain and dreaded the long journey to Cornwall, where we were to stay for the rest of our honeymoon.

On our arrival in St. Ives we found the hotel filled with elderly bridge players. As we entered the dining room on the first evening, a large overwhelming woman descended on us and said, "You must be Gwen Phillipps' daughter! We saw your photo in the paper, my dear. Do come and join us."

This was kind of her, but not very thoughtful. We were on our honeymoon and tired after a long journey. I had no idea who she was and it required much tact to get out of the invitation. The honeymoon was short, as I had to be back at work in five days, but in the circumstances this was really a blessing. We returned to Oxford, Robert to work at the Radcliffe Infirmary where he was still a medical student, and I to Blenheim Palace, MI5 and Roger Hollis.

Chapter 10

Living in Oxford

For the first year after we were married we lived in two rooms in Canterbury Road in Oxford. They were let to us by a crotchety old woman who spent her time writing notices of instruction and sticking them up around the house. One on the lavatory door, for example, read "DO NOT PULL THE CHAIN WITH A JERK OR A BANG." We realised, too, that she went through the contents of our wastepaper basket, when we found an old visiting card belonging to Robert's father on the hall table. It had been cleaned up (and even possibly ironed) and left there to suggest to visitors that Sir Percy and Lady Fynn had, at some time, visited her establishment!

The kitchen, which we shared with two other families, was tiny and at the end of the upstairs passage, underneath a sloping roof. Robert could not even stand up in it. We had a small sitting room and bedroom into which we had to unload all our possessions, food and cooking utensils. Each morning Robert cycled to the Radcliffe Infirmary and I caught the bus to Blenheim. We ate at weekends in the 'British Restaurant' run by the Government, where you could get a first and second course meal for ninepence: it was boring, but convenient and cheap. I was paid three pounds ten shillings a week and Robert, still a student, relied on £50 a year, which was all that his mother could afford to send him. Where we would have been without my father's contribution of £60 a year I do not know, although with both of us working seven days a week we had little time to spend money.

I remained working for Roger Hollis at MI5 until I found that I was pregnant. Then, in the late autumn of 1943, I moved to the Inter Service Topographical Department in Mansfield College where the hours were easier and I could bike to work. I became secretary to David Letts who was the contact with the RAF at Medmenham, where all Coastal Command reconnaissance photographs were collected and sent on to various centres. This made me feel that I had a closer connection with Hugh, who had died flying with Coastal Command.

Much of our map work in this department was assisted by an appeal which had been sent out asking anyone with holiday snaps or postcards of the European coastline, or of other coasts in different parts of the world, to send them to a certain address. Many were received, and although some of the photographs were obscured by figures in the foreground which obliterated the vital landmarks, others helped greatly in the drafting of the final coastal maps which went with the invasion craft when, at last, the final phase of the war began. It would have been good if we could have thanked those who assisted in this way and told them just how they had helped to win the war, but secrecy was paramount.

The office was 'Inter Service', which meant that we were working in close conjunction with the Americans. Night sorties to France were made, initially by submarine and then in rubber dinghies which moved silently towards the coast, in order to assess the quality of the beaches. In the event of an invasion heavy equipment would have to cross beaches to reach the mainland. One day one of the Wrens who worked with us noticed something unusual on a reconnaissance photographic sequence. When she scrutinised the photographs again and again in the following days, the image of a road became more and more positive, although it seemed to be leading nowhere. I remember the excitement we all felt when suddenly she was able to see a large camouflaged area covering what appeared to be a rocket-launching site. Her find enabled the site to be pinpointed and the installation to be wiped out.

Later in the war Robert's brother, Ted, who was in the London Scottish regiment, had been seconded to No. 2 Commando. Men from this unit made reconnaissance trips to the continent under cover of darkness and Ted sometimes armed himself with his favourite weapons, bows and arrows. These were effective and, being silent, had the advantage of preventing his presence from becoming known to the enemy. When he was transferred to Yugoslavia to join Jack Churchill and assist Tito, he left his bows and arrows behind. However, on his return he could not locate them and therefore sent various letters to HQ enquiring for them.

Eventually he went in person, but instead of the weapons he was presented with a large file labelled 'Fynn's Bows and Arrows'. Inside, he found quantities of letters querying the code-words *BOWS AND ARROWS* and asking to what they referred. These enquiries had taken up much time while the file grew in size, and no one had discovered the answer. Ted turned to the officer, who was expecting the revelation of an important secret and said 'Why, it refers to bows and arrows, of course!' By that period of the war we had become so conscious of secrecy that the forces assumed that anything unusual was in code.

Robert was still at the Radcliffe Infirmary studying for his finals and spending most of his time living in at the hospital, but I was coming up to full term in my pregnancy. By now I was not happy in Canterbury Road. However, through my brother-in-law we were able to move.

Ted, who, like Robert, had been a Rhodes Scholar at Oxford, knew a Mrs Haldane, the mother of J.B.S. Haldane and Naomi Mitchison. Mrs Haldane had befriended Ted when he was a student and he put us in touch with her. She was the most delightful old lady and had a large house called 'Cherwell' near the river in North Oxford. At the time we met her she was in her nineties and generously allowed us to have her huge attic as a bed-sitting room. There were many other guests there, most of them from various Government or Service Departments evacuated to Oxford. We ate our evening meals in Mrs Haldane's dining room, where the menu frequently included rabbits sitting rampant upon a large serving dish. They were the last remaining animals from her late husband's experiments concerning the Mendelian Theory. Never before had I seen rabbits served up in this way, sitting up, looking like miniature, eyeless greyhounds ready to spring off the dish. They were most offputting to anyone, let alone to someone in my condition.

The conversation was lively at the table, and once, during a hushed moment, Mrs Haldane overheard a reference made by a guest to J.B.S.'s Communist sympathies. Rising up to her full height of five feet, she banged loudly on the table with a serving spoon and announced, "He is young: he will grow out of it." At this time J.B.S. must have been approaching seventy, for she herself was ninety-five.

On another occasion the conversation concerned war-correspondents and Mrs Haldane remarked that when she was young she had had a lover who was a war-correspondent in the Franco-Prussian War - although of course the word 'lover' did not mean the same thing in her vocabulary as it does today. She told us that he rode all over Europe but never found the war at all. It seems the poor man always reached the war-zone after the battle was over! I have always found these rare occasions fascinating, when one comes across anecdotes which date from the distant past, yet are still alive in the memories of very old people. Now, as I try to complete this autobiography myself, however, I realise that my younger readers will have the same feeling of having jumped back in time, in which case memories of someone alive during the Franco-Prussian War must seem unbelievably ancient.

Chapter 11

A Strange Encounter

The attic in Cherwell was cold and full of discarded furniture from various parts of the house. There was a huge brass bed which was so high that I almost needed a stepladder to get up onto it, while old trunks and other archaic objects were pushed up around the walls. Robert spent most of his time sleeping at the hospital as he was doing midwifery and had to be on the spot. I worked on at the Department until the last few weeks before the baby was due. A specialist, Joe Wrigley from St. Thomas' Hospital, who was a great friend of my father, had offered to deliver the baby, but unfortunately he was taken ill due to an accident in theatre when his eye became infected, so I was handed over to John Stalworthy, who kindly agreed to do a home delivery. In addition I employed a strange little old woman as a nurse, who turned out to know less about babies than I did. She felt sure that I should know whether I was having a boy or a girl as I had had an X-ray, and when I told her that X-rays only showed up bones, she remarked rather illogically that in that case I should certainly have been able to see if it was a boy! Ultrasound scans, of course, had not been invented.

Robert was at home when, in the middle of the night, I realised that things were progressing fairly fast and that he had better phone for Mr Stalworthy. However, he could get no answer to the telephone - we discovered later that he had been ringing Mr Stalworthy's office instead of his home telephone number - and I became more and more distressed. We had no car and ambulances were unobtainable at that period of the war. In the end I begged Robert to ring the police to see if they could get me to the hospital.

At about two o'clock in the morning a charming middle-aged policeman turned up to rescue me. He carted me down from the top of the house over his shoulder and put me into the back of his van. I reached the hospital in one piece only to be met by a tough woman, a sort of assistant nurse, who turned out to be a Christian Scientist. She told me that if I had pain it was my own fault, and then proceeded to examine me. I was so angry with her that with a great effort I burst my waters down the front of her uniform, and in response to that she left me alone on a trolley in a side ward. I could hear Robert's voice down the passage, chatting with the nurses, but had no bell or any way of calling him or anyone else. I was panicking as the pains redoubled their strength and I was afraid that the baby would be born on a trolley with no-one there to deliver it.

Suddenly I was aware of a small, dwarf man in a brown garment coming across the room towards me. I could not see his face clearly, for he wore a hood, but when he stood beside me his head came to the level of my face as I lay on the trolley. While he stayed with me he lifted away the pain, and instilled into my mind thoughts of such importance that the remembrance of them has influenced the rest of my life. I could not translate into words the knowledge he put into my mind. All I knew was that it would remain with me as a 'knowing' until the time when I had developed the wisdom with which to use it.

How long he was with me I do not know. It was as though 'time was away and somewhere else.' As he turned to leave he raised his hand in farewell and at the same moment there was a rush of people into the room. They were horrified to find that I had been left unattended and I was taken straight into theatre and given gas to relieve the pain of the delivery. Although he was in the same hospital, Robert was not at Peter's birth, because in those days men were not expected to attend their wives during childbirth. When I was on the point of delivery, I remember, Mr Stalworthy shouted at the anaesthetist not to stop giving me gas, adding the stock phrase "If the patient can stay awake, why can't you?" Then I passed out for a few moments while Peter was born.

My experience of meeting with the dwarf was to surface again forty-five years later when I was shopping in Exeter one day. I had gone to a book shop with a book-token and had a clear idea of what I wanted. However I seemed to be guided towards another part of the shop and, surprisingly, found myself buying Larousse's *Encyclopaedia of Mythology*.

On my return home I opened the encyclopaedia at random, still without any idea as to why I had bought that particular book. The page before me showed a drawing of an ancient god called 'Bes'. I had never heard of him and had no interest in the subject - or so I thought. However, instead of turning the page, but still in a rather half-hearted way, I started to read the column below the very ugly picture of the little god. Suddenly I was astounded to read that Bes was the dwarf-god of women in labour and childbirth, who had been recorded as appearing at the bedsides of the queens of ancient Sumaria:

> Bes often appeared at birth....we often see Bes represented in the *mammisii* of temples - that is to say, in the birth houses where divine accouchements took place. He thus presided over childbearing and at Deir el Bahri he appears...beside the queen's bed as a protector of expectant mothers.

There, before me, was the identity of the caring dwarf who had appeared at my bedside in the labour ward of the Radcliffe Infirmary. In spite of the passing of the years, the occasion had often been in my thoughts. I now found that he was not just a figment of my imagination, but a beloved and revered domestic god recorded in the history of the ancient Sumarians and Egyptians; a god who had helped women in childbirth for thousands of years.

In 1990, while on holiday in Egypt, I hoped to find a carving of Bes which I had heard could be seen on a pillar of the temple at Philae. The charming Nubian professor who was escorting our group had not heard of Bes but was intrigued by my experience. He managed to arrange for me to be admitted to the place of birthing in the temple, where ancient queens and noblewomen were brought to deliver their children, and there we found Bes carved on a pillar.

Disbelievers have told me that I must have known of Bes before my experience of meeting the dwarf, but this could not have been so. I had not studied the relevant period of ancient history when I was at school, I did not have any idea who he was when he appeared, and never once since then have I met anyone who has heard of a dwarf-god called Bes. That I bought the encyclopaedia which gave me his history might be seen as a coincidence, but to me it is a *synchronicity*, a discovery into which I was led in order that our distant meeting could be revived and valued in a new way. I found out that the little man I saw was not a fairytale dwarf, but Bes, an ancient domestic god, reverenced by people for thousands of years.

There is so much to think about concerning this event: the meaning of 'myth', the strange absence of 'time' while in the presence of the god, his power to remove pain, and the experience of dimensions of which we have no knowledge. It remains in my mind as a wonder of wonders, a moment of extreme joy, a gift of ancient truth.

Chapter 12

Motherhood

There was no room at the Radcliffe Infirmary for me to remain there so I was sent home with my baby in an ambulance the same day. The ambulance men carried us both upstairs in a chair-lift and the babe and I collapsed into bed. Only then did I have a moment in which to hold and examine my beautiful child.

My mother came down from London the next day and was delighted with her first grandchild, although her immediate comment was "Thank God he is white!" Unknown to me, she had been concerned by the thought that many white South African families had black blood in their veins and that, through Robert's genes, my baby might be coloured. I told her that I wanted to christen our baby Peter, after my brother who had died, but that I would not do so if she did not agree. She thought about it and then seemed delighted. Perhaps it laid to rest the memory of her child's death when she was able to hold her first grandson.

Peter was born in May 1944, and in the same year Robert qualified as a doctor and was sent to the outskirts of London to work in a clearing station which dealt with the many casualties caused by continuing air-raids. I stayed in Oxford with Peter, as I dared not take him into danger. Eventually, however, Robert was called up into the Royal Army Medical Corps (the RAMC) and was granted embarkation leave in March 1945. The war in Europe was drawing to a close but there was still much going on in the Far East, so Robert was sent to Bombay, where he was to remain for the rest of the war.

After he left I found that I was pregnant again and, the air-raids having calmed down, I returned to London to stay with my parents. The bombing and V1's were over but there were still V2 rockets falling on London occasionally. After the risks London had been subjected to over the previous few years, the situation in the last year of the war did not seem very dangerous (although in fact the capital narrowly avoided total destruction at this period. We only learned later on how the courage of the commandoes who destroyed the heavy water installations in German-occupied territories had saved Britain from atomic bombs. Apparently the Germans had intended to use atomic warheads in the V2 rockets which fell on London towards the end of the war).

Robert had got on so well with my parents that it had been agreed he would join my father's practice when the war ended. We all thought that this was a marvellous idea as my father had a large practice in Chelsea and was getting on in age. He had been worn out by the long war years working with the Chelsea Mobile Unit as well as in his own private medical practice. I managed to find a charming little maisonette in Cadogan Street and settled in to wait for the arrival of the next baby and the return of Robert from India. We did not seem to have been very much in touch at this time. I kept sending him letters asking him to let me have a list of names for the baby, but I received no answer.

Suddenly in November 1945 a telegram arrived which said

RETURNING RHODESIA ARRANGE JOIN ME ASAP STOP

I was horrified, for this was contrary to all that we had planned for the future. My parents were very upset, particularly as my father really needed Robert's assistance after all he had been through during the London Blitz. I wondered whether Robert had forgotten that I was going to have a baby in a month's time and therefore could not, under any circumstances, travel for another few months. Even after the birth, it would still be difficult. Travelling to Africa by ship, alone and with two infants under two years old plus all our worldly goods, would not have been easy at the best of times. My mind was overwhelmed with all the reasons why such a move was unthinkable, but as Robert was at sea, returning from Bombay to Durban, I was unable to get in touch with him.

The next few weeks were filled with worry and depression at the thought that all our plans had been overthrown. My daughter Sally was delivered in a London nursing home just before Christmas, and I returned to Cadogan Street and promptly went down with the serious type of influenza which was epidemic at the end of the war. My mother employed a young girl to help her to look after Peter in their flat, and a nanny to look after Sally and me in Cadogan Street. I even became so ill that she also had to find a nurse for a while. The maisonette was so small, however, with only three tiny bedrooms, that the nurse could not be resident, but had to come in by the day.

Having flu so soon after having a baby meant that I did not recover very quickly and it was not until March 1946 that I began to feel strong enough to consider the future. My mother would have loved to persuade me to stay in England until Robert could return to fetch me, but I was sure that he hadn't the money to be able to do such a thing. If I were to join him in Rhodesia, however, the army would arrange my passage as part of *his* demobilisation to his home country. Reluctantly I began to pack up our wedding presents and household items, the pram, cots and nappies, and clothing for the babies as well as myself. I had been warned that when the notice came for me to embark I would be given very little time to prepare.

Chapter 13

A Devastating Journey

It was late in April 1946 that I was notified that my time for embarkation would be early in May. Ted's wife, Viv, had taken over a previous passage allotted to me which had been booked for the beginning of February, for at that time I was still too ill to leave. She and her baby, Robin, had had a pretty disastrous start to the voyage as the ship had broken down in the Bay of Biscay and had been forced to return to England for repairs. The weather had been terrible and the ship had sat out at sea for days before setting off again. The passage in May was my last chance to be sent to Africa as a 'returning' army wife and family (although of course, my children and I were not really *returning*, having never been to Rhodesia!) I was to sail from Liverpool in two weeks' time on the SS *Umgeni*.

I was devastated at leaving England, the family, my little house and my life and I was also deeply worried, as there was still danger from mines at sea. At that time I seemed to have no pioneering spirit, only an overwhelming desire to remain safely in one place with those I loved. My mother was too distressed to come to Liverpool with me, still feeling that Robert should have returned to help me on the journey. However, he had already arrived in Rhodesia, penniless it seemed, and he wrote that it was out of the question.

My sisters, Christine and Stella, nobly took on the job of helping me to get ready to travel. All our possessions had to be crated, and prams and cots and all the other paraphernalia necessary when travelling with two infants, had to be sorted and labelled 'Wanted on Board' or 'Hold'. The large double pram was filled with nappies, not the easy sort we have nowadays, but washable terry-towelling and Harrington squares. I said a sad farewell to my mother and father, my brothers and sister Chris at the station in London, while Stella travelled by train to Liverpool with me and was the greatest blessing. I had no idea what was to happen when I reached Capetown, and indeed had I known what was eventually to happen, I believe I would never have left.

We stayed the night in a huge hotel and at the crack of dawn, unable to raise the hotel service, Stella raided the early-morning tea trays all down the passage in order to collect enough milk for the babies. Peter was not yet two and Sally was five months old and together they were going to be far too much for me to cope with alone on a three-week-long journey on a small, overcrowded ship.

When we reached the berth where the *SS Umgeni* lay we were told that no visitors, only passengers, were allowed on board. I burst into tears, but Stella said, "Rubbish" and marched through the barrier carrying one baby. No-one stopped her so I followed with the other baby and we found our way to a two-berth cabin which had been fitted up with two additional bunks. I was to share the cabin with another woman and her child. The other mother was an RAF widow, Molly Guest, who was taking her son to Rhodesia to visit her husband's parents. She must have been shattered to see so many of us piling into the small space in which we were all to live for the next three weeks. Stella stayed as long as she could, but bells rang and she had to go. She told me later that she had felt awful at leaving me in such circumstances on such a small ship, in a cramped, chaotic space, when she knew how reluctant I was to leave and how likely I was to suffer from sea-sickness.

The voyage was not really too bad, and would have been quite reasonable had I not had so much to do. Nappy-washing took up much of my time and had to be done in cold salt water, which did not do the babies' bottoms any good. I hardly ever managed to get to the dining room for a meal. Children had to eat separately from the adults and by the time I had fed Peter in the children's dining room, strapped him into the pram on deck while I went to the kitchen to get boiling water to make up Sally's feed, and then fed her, the main dining room had closed. I lived on the scraps which were left over after the children's meals.

By the evening I was exhausted but could not leave the children alone in the cabin at night to take a break. Visiting the kitchens across the way to get boiling water to make up Sally's bottles in the night was a nightmare, for when I opened the kitchen door the whole floor rose up and scuttled away from me. I have never seen so many cockroaches. They crunched under my feet as I made my way across to the stove and it was a test of courage to handle anything which might have been walked over by them. The very fact of bringing a baby's bottle into such a place filled me with disgust.

The two little boys, Molly's son Johnnie and my son Peter, did not get on, and were too small to be trusted to stay in the cabin alone. The decks were dangerous, for the railings were too far apart for safety and there were wide gaps around the lifeboats where a child could fall straight into the sea. Lifeboat drill happened frequently and there were strict rules about lifejackets and clothing to be taken to the boats. If, when the alarm was sounded, Peter was in his pram on deck and Sally in her cot in the cabin several decks below, I had to rush down to get her, fetch my lifejacket and her food, bottles and clothes, return to the deck to fetch Peter (who was by that time hysterical at the noise of the alarms) and then find the woman from the next cabin who had offered to take Sally with her, as I could not get two little children inside my lifejacket. By the time I reached my boat station the rehearsal was always over. I do not think that our hopes of survival would have been good if the ship was sinking.

The only area where the children were allowed to play was on the boat deck and the Captain was not sympathetic about the danger the children were in from the gaps in the ship's railings. We eventually managed to get the crew to rig up a netted playpen in the centre of the deck into which we put all the children. Some children had toys and some did not and there were constant fights. If I had to go down to cope with the baby, I had to strap Peter into the large pram, which I had roped onto a seat on the deck. There he would sit and weep until my return. The voyage upset him badly and he took a long time to regain his confidence when, after much tribulation, we eventually reached Rhodesia.

We reached the island of Gran Canaria and had a few hours to go ashore in the town of Las Palmas. I managed to arrange for the children to be looked after while they were asleep, and I left the ship for a while in the evening. Some of us went to watch a pelota game and got stranded on the island as there were no taxis to take us back to the docks. The ship's siren was blaring and I was in a panic in case the ship was going to sail without me. (I learned later that the Captain could not be found, lost somewhere in the brothels of the town, and that the siren was to summon him. In the end he was brought on board in the early hours of the morning, much the worse for wear, and did not appear again for the rest of the voyage. The poor first officer, who was only twenty-one, had to take charge until we reached Capetown).

During the long stretch between the Canary Islands and the Cape I made a few friends, including a man called John Bowden, who helped enormously on the voyage by carrying babies and carry-cots up and down the companionways for me. He remained a friend for many years afterwards.

The sight of Capetown is always impressive, with Table Mountain rising behind the city. My spirits rose as the voyage came to an end and I looked forward to seeing Robert waiting on the quay to help me for the rest of the journey. The train journey was going to be exhausting, for we still had another thousand miles to travel north from Capetown to Salisbury, capital city of Southern Rhodesia.

As the ship came slowly into her berth, I looked in vain for Robert's tall figure. John was beside me and we were worried that there was no sign of anyone I knew on the dock. However, with the help of John and several caring friends I got ashore, and once there sat on my luggage surrounded by packing cases, trunks and suitcases, together with prams and cots containing the babies, and watched out for Robert's arrival.

Chapter 14

Africa - A Traumatic Arrival

I waited. No one came. Time went by, the babies cried and I cried. I could not leave them or the baggage to find out what to do. Everyone had left the ship and there was no help available. I had no idea how to find a station or the train which was to have taken me north across Africa, or what to do with the mountains of luggage which surrounded me. Time passed and not even an agent turned up.

At last, John came back from his hotel to find out if I was all right. He was deeply concerned to find that no one had come to meet me and proceeded to cope with everything. He found an agent to take over all the baggage and took me and the children to the Mount Nelson Hotel where he and his family were staying. When I had calmed down a bit he asked me why on earth I was going to join someone who could not even arrange for me to be met, and why I did not change my plans and stay with him. Considering what he would have been taking on, I saw this as a very noble gesture. I was tempted to take him up on the offer, but the fact that both he and I were married made it simpler to refuse!

As we discussed the predicament I was in, I became very angry and finally decided not to go on to Rhodesia but to ring my Aunt Molly in Johannesburg and ask her if I could stay with her. I had not seen her since the time, six years before, when I had helped her to pack for her journey to South Africa after the outbreak of war. I did not know whether she would be at home or able to have us so suddenly. John went off to ring her up and came back to say that she was delighted, and he put me on the train with the babies that evening. He had managed to get me a two berth compartment to myself, which was a miracle. As we travelled up the Garden Route, along the east coast of South Africa, Peter played with water in the hand-basin in the compartment and I hung out the washing on strings stretched from the upper bunk on which Sally slept in her carry-cot.

On our arrival we were immediately taken into the heart of a very caring family and Peter, whose second birthday had occurred on the ship, rushed down the platform to my aunt thinking that she was my mother and calling her 'Gan Gan'. It was a great relief to know that the children were in safe hands, as I was not well for the next two weeks. I had a 'breakdown' and was kept in bed. The children were fine but Molly rang Robert to tell him that I was in no state to travel any further alone. She said that if he wanted me to come to Rhodesia he had better come down to fetch me.

Finally after some weeks he arrived and we set off on the last lap of the journey, although, understandably, this was not a good way to meet again after such a disjointed marriage and such a long time apart. The shock of having to leave England, the journey, Robert's failure to make any arrangements for me to be met in Capetown and the fact that we had been apart for fourteen months all conspired to make our meeting a disaster. I was still angry that Robert had accepted a passage back to Rhodesia from India instead of returning to England, and at the way he had treated my father, who had been very generous in offering him a partnership. Added to this, our future in Rhodesia looked bleak, with no house to live in and no prospect of being able to afford to buy one.

The train we boarded took us north through what was then Bechuanaland and this gave me my first fascinating glimpse of tribal life in Africa, and the exuberance and artistic abilities of the African people, particularly the children. They thronged the train at all the stopping places with wood carvings and tin toys made from cans and fencing wire. I was glad to see that many people were keen to buy their artistic efforts.

On our arrival in Salisbury, because we had no home to go to, Robert's elderly mother had to take us in. She, poor woman, had already had two other daughters-in-law arriving on her doorstep with children, and it must have been daunting to have it happen all over again. I could see no hope of ever getting a place of our own, although Robert was sure that we could buy a house without any down-payment. Needless to say this turned out to be a forlorn hope. Our entire assets consisted of £57, and that had to be spent on an old Chevrolet pickup van for Robert to use for his medical practice.

I had left my parent's home in London, which was not lavish, but extremely comfortable with beautiful furniture, and also my little house in Cadogan Street, which I had come to love, and was now faced with living in the house which my parents-in-law had built as pioneers in 1896. It had a tin roof and was drab in the extreme. 'Mother', as she hoped I would call her, believed in having black-painted ceilings to discourage the flies, navy blue walls up to shoulder height to minimise fingermarks, and dark cream paint above. The curtains in our room were navy blue and the floors were stained brown boards, which had been attacked by white ants in many places. 'Mother' was a dear and I grew very fond of her, but she could be quite a tyrant and dealt harshly with her African servants who, in spite of this, seemed to respect her. I was shocked by the way she treated them, and tried to shield the little nurse-girl I employed, who was a great help with the washing and ironing. There was also a charming little boy called Pembere, one of the sons of the cook, who came hopefully one morning to ask if he could help to 'look after the little Boss.' Peter was delighted to have someone to play with, and they got on very well. Pembere was about seven years old and Peter, being only two, respected him and did what he was told. The African word 'Pembere' means 'to go forward' and I sincerely hope he has, for by now he must be a man of sixty-eight or so.

My hopeless longing for a house of our own continued for months, and then a miracle happened. One morning I opened a letter from my grandmother in Jersey and found a cheque for what I first read as £40, then £400 and then, amazingly, £4000. I had never seen so many noughts in my life, for in 1946 four thousand pounds was a great deal of money. It bought us a fully furnished house on five acres of land on Mount Pleasant Drive to the north of Salisbury, and left enough over for a second-hand car and many essentials. The house we had found cost us £2,500, and had an iron roof on top and white ants (termites) underneath!

The relief of our move was enormous both to me and, I am sure, to my mother-in-law. She remained a great friend until her death many years later.

Chapter 15

A Home of Our Own

The house we bought, called 'Inverurie', was not the house of one's dreams but it was in a perfect position on the top of Mount Pleasant Hill overlooking the *commonage* (the green belt around Salisbury). When eventually Mount Pleasant Drive was tarred, the house became easily accessible, but until then the road was a pattern of deep potholes which became small ponds in the rainy season. To drive up and down required much concentration and dexterity.

The house was a bungalow with a corrugated iron roof, more or less square in layout, surrounded by a veranda of cracked, red polished concrete. On entering the hall, which was paved with red hexagonal cement tiles in mock terracotta, you could see through to the land at the back of the house, across a mosquito-netted back verandah. The sitting room and one bedroom were on the left and our bedroom and the dining room were on the right. The kitchen and bathroom were at each end of the back verandah. Our bedroom was furnished with enormous dark wooden wardrobes and a large bed, while the sitting room had a suite of heavy sofas and chairs in a dark leatherette fabric with flat, polished, wooden armrests on which to place beer glasses and 'sundowners'. There was also a terrible orange and brown carpet in the sitting room. I do not think that I could have found anything which was more contrary to my personal taste but at the time the joy at having a place of our own overrode everything else.

Along one side of the house was a small verandah room where we stored many things, until later we discovered that there was a vast white ants' nest under the coconut matting which covered the floor. Clearly the house was in a bad state.

The house had been built on one corner of the five acres, close to the road, which was a blessing because after about five years it enabled us to build another house in a better position, and later on to halve the property and sell off Inverurie with two and a half acres of land. The house we built was called 'Shotover' (after the place of the same name in England) and remained our home for the rest of our time in Africa.

Robert had joined the medical practice of Sir Godfrey Huggins (later to become Lord Malvern). It was a fairly large group of surgeons and general practitioners. Sir Godfrey was the Prime Minister of Southern Rhodesia as well as a doctor and it was said that if you visited him you had to make the purpose of your visit very clear, or you could find yourself being given a prescription instead of political advice, and *vice versa*. By the time Robert joined the practice Sir Godfrey had little to do with it, all his time being taken up with the mounting political problems which were beginning to threaten the country in the wake of the recent war in Europe.

Robert was engaged on the understanding that he would become a junior partner at the end of five years. In the event this did not happen, and at the end of seven years disagreements reached such a pitch that the medical group disintegrated, and Robert found himself taking over the consulting rooms with the other general practitioners. This was a great advantage to him, however, and his practice flourished.

Soon after we had bought 'Inverurie', I borrowed two hundred pounds from my brother Ian in England and set about building a cottage at the far end of the five acres. It was constructed of treated gum poles set into the earth, and roofed with deep thatch, the roof being very large and sloping down to low eaves. The walls between the gum poles were made of mud and grass, pressed into wire netting stretched between the poles, and the wall was then plastered on both sides with more mud to a thickness of about three inches. The cottage was whitewashed inside and out, while the poles were stained dark brown, and the effect was good. Inside, the cottage had a fairly big central sitting room with two small rooms on each side. The front door opened into the sitting room, two of the small rooms were used as bedrooms, one was a bathroom and the fourth was a tiny dining area which had a back door opening towards the kitchen. This was outside and was roofed with sheet tin for the sake of safety. All this was built for less than two hundred pounds by unskilled labour overseen by myself, and I let it for several years for a small personal income which was helpful.

The tenants who rented the cottage were not always very suitable, however. One rather striking woman was found by Robert. The position appealed to her because it was out of the city and fairly secluded, but we discovered that we had taken on a lady of ill-repute. Our neighbours came round and told us that there was a different car there every night and, as some of these cars belonged to people they knew, it was embarrassing. I summoned up the courage to go and tell her that she could not stay, but she saw me coming and told me she was moving.

When we eventually decided to divide the five acres and sell 'Inverurie' we had to sell the cottage as well. However when I returned to Rhodesia nearly forty years later I found my cottage still in good condition surrounded by a pretty garden.

We sold 'Inverurie' and half its land to friends, the Cootes, but in the time it took to build 'Shotover' on the other two and a half acres, they lived happily in my little cottage. Houses were in very short supply after the war and they had agreed to wait until the building of our house was completed. I was delighted to think that the £200 the cottage had cost me had been well spent.

'Shotover' was finished several months later and was a great success. We discovered that we had built on a bit of property which had been owned by one of Robert's elderly uncles many years before. Uncle Mev was a charming old man who had camped in many places in Africa during his life, and, at eighty years old, had still not settled down. He owned an old 'Chev' pick-up van, the roof of which he had thatched when the original one rusted away. He drove his car steadily at about twenty miles an hour with straw flying off the roof, stopping for nothing, not even red lights or policemen. Once he hit a row of poles which held up a verandah of a shop in Salisbury, and went off to the nearest pub for a drink to steady his nerves before going to the police station to report the accident!

He shocked us one day when he arrived at our house and informed us that we should be careful when we were digging in the garden as several of his little children were buried there. I was horrified, but my mother-in-law told me not to worry. She said that as far as she could remember his wife had had a miscarriage at the end of the last century, but apart from that she was sure there were no other burials. When Uncle Mev left us he drove off to Enkledoorn with a load of chickens in the back of his car, for he had heard that he could get sixpence apiece more for the chickens down there than he had paid for them in Salisbury. We did not remind him of the cost of the petrol and the wear and tear to his almost derelict car.

Chapter 16

Anton Chikopa

In February 1949 our third child, Richard, was born at the Lady Chancellor Nursing Home in Salisbury. Robert found a friend of his to come and look after Peter and Sally and I came home with Richard within forty-eight hours. He was a wonderfully good baby and life went on peacefully. His nanny, Theresa, was a charming African girl who, although untrained, took to instruction very well. There was always tension between the African men and any girls employed in domestic work, however, because for some reason the men felt that it was their right to work in the house. This attitude changed over the years and in recent times many more women were employed in domestic work.

It was at this time that Anton Chikopa first came to work for us as cook. He became a great friend in spite of a tendency to drink too much beer before every dinner party. His drinking was caused by worry in case things did not go right, but it resulted in making things far more difficult for us and for himself. There were many occasions when Robert sacked him the following morning and I had to smooth things over in order to reinstate him before the evening. He was always very apologetic and begged to be kept on, as he loved his work and the family.

Anton liked to spring surprises on us, and one Christmas he brought a large dish to the table with a cover over it. I could not imagine what it was, and his face was a picture as he set it down before Robert, whipped off the cover and revealed a huge, live tortoise sitting on the plate. He had found it in the garden and thought that the children would be delighted. Unfortunately it had a telephone number painted in red on its back and I had to return it to its owner.

Few of the Africans who worked for us had any previous experience and few of them could read. Added to this was the fact that it was necessary for me to learn a very basic language with which to communicate with my employees. It was neither English nor African, but a kind of universally-accepted invented language or pidgin which included words from various languages and from Afrikaans.

Communication could often be difficult. I remember my mother-in-law telling me of a dinner party which she attended with her husband. The hostess was very particular and had taken a lot of trouble, instructing her cook to roast a sucking pig and to cook various vegetables. Realising that he was going to have a lot to do she asked whether his small son could carry in the pig on its dish. She told him to garnish the pig by placing an apple in the mouth and parsley behind the ears. When the main course was due the door was opened to allow a very small black boy to enter. The dish was hot and he had lifted up his shirt, his only garment, in order to protect his hands. There was a stunned silence as he staggered to the table with the dish, for the boy had an apple in his mouth and parsley over his ears!

One day Anton came to me and said that his wife was 'frighted' and would have to go back to Nyasaland. I asked him why she was afraid and he told me the following story. He said, "There is a man with a big truck who come at night and point a big white stick at you and you go stiff like a tree and he make you walk into his truck. He take you away and make you into beef and put you in a tin."

I said, "Anton, you cannot believe that. The police would never allow such a thing," to which he replied, "The police they know but they say to take only one or two natives in each place and they will not notice."

I asked him who had told him this story and he said that many natives knew it was true. I said, "You don't believe it yourself do you?" and he replied, "Not me, I am educated native. I do not believe...but it could happen."

Anton's wife went back to Nyasaland, and although he stayed he was very apprehensive. I was aware that there were troublemakers at large in the country, stirring up the African people, but it was not easy to find out where such rumours originated. A few days later, in the local store, I came across a tin of Argentine beef which was sold for African consumption. To my amazement it had the face of an African man on the label. I bought it and took it back home and into the kitchen. Anton jumped back in horror when he saw it, looked grey and kept exclaiming "A! A! A!" a typical African expression indicating fear.

I told him that the label said that the meat in the tin came from a country hundreds of miles away and was beef from a bull, but still he could not touch the tin. He said, "Madam, when you buy little fish in a tin there is a picture of the little fish on the tin, when there is a fruit in a tin there is a picture of a fruit, and oh! Madam, you have a tin in the cupboard which has a big blue bird on it. I am wanting you to open it so that I can see the blue bird." I told him that the tin contained pears and opened it to show him. I hoped that this would convince him that having a black face on a tin of beef did not mean that the meat inside came from a black man. He remained only half convinced and insisted that I remove the tin from the house.

Anton was an excellent cook. He could remember every recipe I taught him and never made a mistake, for although he could not read or write he was extremely intelligent. In spite of this he thought it was quite possible that a man with a stick could point it at a person and cause them to go "stiff like a tree" and walk into a truck to be killed. He stayed with us for many years and his son came to help as well. When he finally retired to Nyasaland I failed to find anyone half as reliable. I never heard from him again, but of course there was no way that he could personally have sent a letter. I can only hope that he was all right, and I feel sure that he would have contacted us somehow if he had been in need.

Anton was a small man and had Egyptian features and was quite unlike the other Bantu. We wondered whether his ancestors were possibly ancient slave-traders who had invaded the east coast of Africa in past centuries. The mountains of Inyanga were dotted with so-called 'slave pits' and it was believed by some that these pits were used as resting places where slaves could be held when the slavers stopped on their way to the coast. Others believed that they were for very small cattle or goats. I suspect that it will never be known what the reason was for their presence along the route from Central Africa to the East coast, but personally I am inclined to think that the slave trade was involved.

Chapter 17

Inyanga Holidays and Life At Shotover

When Robert was a student he had bought about twenty acres of land in the mountains of Inyanga, for which he had paid five shillings an acre. We now set about planning a holiday cottage up there. This was a lengthy business as it was more than two hundred miles away and the road was a 'strip road' for three-quarters of the way and an unmade rough mountain track from there on. Strip roads were common all over the country at that time and were the only way to get about in the rainy season. They were both a blessing and a curse for they could become very dangerous. They were built with two concrete strips set apart at the width of the wheelbase of cars and trucks. There was little traffic, which was a good thing, because when you met a car coming the other way there was only one way for the two cars to pass each other. Both cars had to get off the left-hand strip onto the side of the road and get their right-hand wheels onto the vacated strip. The result of this was that the centre between the strips became hollowed out, and the road to the left-hand side of the concrete strips wore away. Your wheels could fall into cavities on either side, which was both dangerous and hard on the walls of the tyres. If the passing manoeuvre had to be undertaken in a hurry, as it sometimes did, the vehicle was liable to go out of control.

When the strips came to an end at the foot of the mountains, driving became even harder. The dust of Africa has to be experienced to be believed. It is red and covers the windscreen, only subsiding when the rains come - and then the mud is worse. The roads on my journeys up to Inyanga with the children in my old A40 van were sometimes so dangerous that I had to make the children get out and walk. I could then negotiate a particularly badly cambered part of the sandy or muddy mountain road, which sloped towards a sheer drop into a river many feet below. Had I gone over the edge I do not know what the children would have done, but it seemed better not to risk their lives as well as mine. More often than not we made the journey without Robert, as he was busy working.

Our builder in Inyanga was a pleasant man and quite good at his job, when he was there. His name was Vanisher and unfortunately he lived up to it. The African caretaker who lived on the spot would meet us with the news that Vanisher had gone and he did not know when he would be back. Having come two hundred miles to bring him materials and to discuss the building with him, I would be furious, especially as I had sent messages to say I was coming.

After much trouble getting the sand and cement up the mountain road, the concrete platform for the cottage was laid and I supervised drums of arsenic being poured into a trench which had been dug all round the perimeter of the foundation and filled with dried grass. This precaution, which must have been very dangerous, was to prevent white ants demolishing the wood in the building which we were about to construct. I cannot imagine that in any other country you would be able to buy large drums of black oily arsenic, but there seemed to be no difficulty in those early days in Rhodesia.

On one occasion we brought up the parts of the lavatory which we set up on one corner of the concrete slab. The walls were not yet built and the pipe waved about with the cistern on top until a gum pole was put up to support it. The wastepipe to the septic tank was installed and the pit dug, and gradually the walls went up and the cottage emerged. It was constructed of badly burnt bricks which were all that we could get hold of locally. Interestingly, the remainder of the bricks, which were left outside at the back of the cottage, dissolved into the earth after a few rainy seasons. However, thanks to the plaster which covered them, the walls survived.

The roof was an enormous undertaking, for the cottage was double-storey and the roof trusses were very wide. Robert had ordered one long length of wood which would be used for the roof tree. It was over thirty feet in length and had taken some while to obtain. Before we returned to Salisbury Robert demonstrated to Vanisher exactly how all this was to be placed. He made one fatal mistake, however, in placing a short piece of wood into the notch in the top of a roof truss to show how the long roof tree would lie along the tops of the trusses. When we returned the roof trusses were up, but were held together only by the thin strips of the slats designed to hold the shingles. The long wooden strip for the roof tree had been carefully cut into short pieces, similar to the one with which Robert had demonstrated, and each piece was fitted into the top of an individual truss. Our 36-foot length of wood no longer existed; there was no roof tree. Such is Africa, but where did the blame lie? Not with the builder, for he obeyed instructions literally, whatever he may have thought of the lack of common sense of the white man.

When the Inyanga cottage was habitable we had many wonderful holidays there on the side of the mountain above the Tsanga River. The cottage still stood when I last heard about it, considerably improved and strengthened by its new owners, but whether it will survive the horrors of present-day Zimbabwe as I write, I do not know.

Our fourth baby, David, was born in September 1951. We had started to build 'Shotover', our house in Salisbury, about two years before. In our application for building permission we had implied that by the time the house was built we would have four children, because building restrictions were very stringent and the square footage you were allowed depended on the number of people in the family. As it was, David *was* there by the time we moved in, but on paper I appeared to have had a twenty-four month pregnancy.

'Shotover' enjoyed the same lovely view that we had had at 'Inverurie', and a little railway line ran below the house. The train would sound its hooter as it ran down the hill to the city, but this was the only warning of its approach and there were many near misses and some fatalities at the various road crossings.

We set about making a garden on two and a half acres of rough ground covered with elephant grass. The going was tough and the gardeners worked hard planting flamboyants, jacarandas, an Australian chestnut, a kapok tree and many other shrubs and smaller trees. When, nearly 25 years later, I returned and was allowed by the new owners to walk round the garden, the trees were huge and I was amazed at how quickly they had grown.

When the children were older we arranged for a swimming pool to be dug. We went away for a couple of weeks to Capetown leaving the hole marked out and expecting to find that it was under way when we got back. On our return we were faced with a mountain of subsoil and an enormous hole. The African builders had excelled themselves, but none of us had realised exactly how much soil would result from their work. The sides of the hole were straight and the depth was pretty accurate. We had left a pole with them as a measure, so that they would know when to stop digging. However, it was not long before the pool was bricked up, sealed and painted and was in constant use, and somehow the subsoil which had been removed in the digging disappeared gradually around various parts of the garden.

One day, some years later, I was looking out of the sitting room window. I watched Richard, then aged about twelve, very thin and long-legged, running naked towards the pool. He took off over the water in a huge leap. In the air he suddenly screamed and back-pedalled with his legs, and although he landed in the pool with a splash he immediately leaped from the water again. He had almost landed on a cobra which he had seen swimming across the pool below him!

We had several encounters with snakes, perhaps the most dangerous one being when Peter was five and came in to tell me that he had seen a black and red snake by the swing under the cedrillatuna trees. I did not take this too seriously, as I could see no sign of where it could have come from and at five years old he could have been imagining things. However, the next day while the children were out, our gardener killed a five-foot banded cobra at the same spot. It had recently shed its skin and was a shiny black and orange colour. I was horrified to think how close it had been to Peter. We wondered whether it could have had a mate, but we saw no sign of it over the following weeks, and the hole in the hedge from which the first snake had come was filled up with rocks.

On another occasion a brown snake was seen by the children going up one of the drain pipes on the side of the house. Peter ran up to the top veranda and pushed it down with a broom-handle and I waited at the bottom of the pipe with a pillowcase to catch it. Peter shouted to me that it was coming down and I placed the pillowcase over the exit. When he said it was in the bag, I closed the top tightly with my fist and withdrew the bag from the downpipe, only to find the snake's head looking straight at me. I shook it down into the bag and we put it into an aquarium with a sheet of glass on the top, while preparing to take it to the snake park. A moment later, while we were watching, the cat walked past the aquarium and the snake rose up, opened its hood and spat venom against the glass. I was a bit shaken to think of the close encounter I had just had, and that it was with a cobra and not just a harmless snake.

When David was fourteen months old I took the children on holiday to Inyanga. Our nanny was also on holiday with her children in a nearby village and I had employed another girl to help with David. One day I was having coffee in the sitting room at a friend's cottage and David, who could only just stand by himself and walk a few steps, was playing with his temporary nanny on the lawn at the back of the house. My friend and I had been chatting over our coffee for a while when I suddenly leaped from my chair and ran from the room, out through the back door and down a long path, and jumped into the middle of a stream which ran along the bottom of the garden. I landed right beside David, who was swimming under the water with only his plastic pants showing like a balloon on the surface. I seemed to come to as I grabbed him, and only then did I realise what had happened.

By some unknown means I had been directed straight to the spot were he was. I had not asked anyone if they had seen him and I had not alerted the nurse girl, whom we later found in an alcoholic stupor up by the kitchen, having been given kaffir-beer by the cook. No-one had realised that there was anything amiss and David himself could have only just reached the water, for he was happily submerged, floating along towards a waterfall. Had I come out to fetch him later on, and had we started to look for him only then, he would certainly have drowned.

I realised that the tragedy had been averted by some intervention which I did not understand, but I could not explain this to the other people who were there. They had been surprised at my sudden rush from the room, but had not questioned it until I appeared with a soaking wet child. David had apparently been enjoying his swim until I grabbed him from the water, after which he began to howl. I realised that he had not breathed in any water and was perfectly all right. The lawn on which he had had to travel to reach the stream sloped in several stages down to the water, which was quite a long way from where he had been sitting on a rug with the nurse girl. In order to have reached the water he must have crawled and rolled (and perhaps walked a little) down the slopes for quite a distance, but - judging from where he was in the stream when I reached him - he could only have been approaching the water and not yet in it at the time I was alerted.

In later years further strange things happened in my life, one in particular also resulting in the saving of a child's life, but at the time of saving David I was not able to come to terms with the strangeness of the event. It seemed as if there had been some form of spirit intervention which had numbed my mind so that I followed the directions of my instructor and did not attempt to use my own brain to search for David. If I had, I believe that I would have been too late.

Chapter 18

1955 - The Inyanga Experience

David's life having been saved by some power beyond my understanding, I became more aware of various strange events which had taken place in the past. I had been having dreams of great significance but it was a year or two later that a life-changing encounter took place in full daylight up in the mountains of Inyanga. What follows here is from the account which I tried to write at the time:

I had gone down to the river to call the children back for lunch and I sat down briefly on a rock looking towards the distant mountains of Portuguese East Africa (now Mozambique) which showed in a blue haze on the horizon. My marriage was becoming harder and harder to accept and I was deeply unhappy and homesick. The words of Keats came into my mind and I thought of

> *Perhaps the self-same song that found a path*
> *Through the sad heart of Ruth, when sick for home*
> *She stood in tears amid the alien corn.*

The homesickness which had engulfed me for so long had become a part of my life, and while appreciating the majesty of Africa, my thoughts wandered as usual to the shores of England, her small villages and the beauty of her countryside; I mourned the separation from my parents and the rest of my family. There, under the waves, somewhere unknown off the south coast of England, lay the remains of my love. I had suffered permanent pain since receiving that one word "Missing" so many years before.

The roar of the waterfall and the shouting of the children, as they slid down the rockface below me, fell silent. I no longer felt the throbbing heat of the African sun, and it was as if I had been lifted into total silence. I had left my normal body, yet my mind was able to sense the reassurance of a myriad of what appeared to be butterfly wings, fanning the air about me. I was no longer alone and as I moved into a space above the river, a mist rose enclosing me within a circle, in the centre of which was a living movement of light, a light so penetrating, that I can only liken it to white fire which grew more intense as I watched.

It seemed to clothe a power beyond all understanding, which I can only give the name of *It*. I was attracted to It as if by a magnet, my mind receiving knowledge which later I was to recall as words, but which, at the time, seemed to enter me wordlessly from a great and powerful Wisdom. Indeed, there are no words to express the 'knowing' which was gifted to me in that absence of time.

I finally came to myself back on the rock: the waterfall still roared below me, the children shouted from the river, and the mountains were visible in the far distance.

Time had stood still.

I had no knowledge or religion which would account for the event. For sixteen years, after experiencing the death of Hugh, I had believed that I had lost the touch of God. I had no idea what to make of this recent experience and began to wonder about the possibility of sunstroke. Finally I attempted to make a pact with the unknown power: to show me It really existed, I bargained, It would act again in some way within two months so that I would know and accept It in truth. Then I rose from the rock and called the children up for lunch.

Two months to the day, when I was least expecting to receive any confirmation of the pact made in the Inyanga mountains, an unrecognised voice spoke on the telephone and events were set in motion which changed my life. As a result of the conversation on the telephone, and by a series of further events, I met the man who was to become my spiritual director. To him I was able to express all that I have written above, and to pass on the essence of the knowledge I had received. From him I was given the advice that, for the time being, I should keep it all within my heart, as it was too precious to be discussed with those who might not value it.

Years passed before I was able to use words to transmit the message I had received to anyone else. It seemed that I would damage or destroy its truth if I used common language in the telling, yet there was no other way and such wisdom is not meant to be hidden and guarded for ever. It has to risk ridicule and disbelief, and the messenger has to accept the misreading of the message by many and the understanding of it by only a few. So to the best of my ability, and in spite of the inadequacy of language, I wrote in words the message given into my mind by the power which manifested Itself within the Light:

All love comes from me and returns to me.
You could not love without my gift of love.

All love is mine, given to all.
I AM LOVE.

It was from that moment that I was able to see the love between Hugh and myself as a gift to us both which I must use in my life on his behalf as well as my own.

Chapter 19

Gonville ffrench-Beytagh

My first meeting with Gonville ffrench-Beytagh, the Dean of Salisbury Cathedral in Rhodesia, came about because of a mutual friend of ours called Moyra who had been killed in an air crash. She had been travelling to England with her adopted daughter when the plane crashed at Bengazi. The little girl, aged four, was thrown from the aircraft and was the only survivor of the crash. She was taken to the hospital in Benghazi.

At the time Moyra's husband was with Robert and some other people on an expedition down the Zambezi from Kariba to Beira, to commemorate the centenary of Livingstone's voyage down that river. It proved extremely difficult to find their party, as they were somewhere in the wilds of Portuguese East Africa, but the expedition was eventually located and Michael was lifted off a sandbank by plane and flown immediately to the hospital in Benghazi.

Gonville ffrench-Beytagh had been a great friend of Moyra's and I had to see him about some matter concerning the accident, but as it turned out the meeting was highly significant for me personally. After I had finished telling him of the matter I had come about, I found myself saying, "I think I ought to come and see you some time." When Gonville suggested the following day I immediately backtracked, not knowing why I had mentioned a meeting, but he insisted that it would be a good thing, and as I left he put his hand on my shoulder and said "Bless your heart." In that moment, amazingly, my heart was blessed.

The sense of blessing was totally unexpected and was a profound experience. It was by Gonville's act of blessing that I was able to recall the pact I had made on the mountain in Inyanga; the two months had passed and the reply had been given to me. The next day I plucked up my courage and kept the appointment with Gonville, and so began one of the greatest friendships of my life, one which has influenced my way of living, my thinking and much that has happened to me since.

Gonville Aubie ffrench-Beytagh was an unusual character. Books have been written about him and by him, concerning his childhood and the circumstances of his entering the church, a decision which, in the context of his background, seemed most unlikely. He was born in Shanghai, but when his parents parted his mother went to live in South Africa, leaving the three children with their father in China. Gonville's father soon decided to send the children back to England with their governess, who was instructed to "put them in a Home." The governess, who must have been a remarkable woman, refused to abandon them and raised money from their relatives to keep them with her in England.

At the age of sixteen Gonville was sent to New Zealand to work on a sheep farm. The life was wrong for him, however, and he disliked it so much that he decided to abscond from the farm school. He managed to raise enough money to do this, and with the help of a friend travelled to South Africa in search of his mother, although when he got there he could not find her: she had remarried several times and he did not know her name!

He had landed penniless in Durban and inevitably got into bad hands, was mugged and ended up in hospital where he was found by Alan Paton, the writer, who had made it his work to find and help the many down-and-outs in and around Durban. A great friendship grew up between them and this resulted in Gonville meeting Archbishop Clayton in Capetown. Gonville told Clayton that he believed he had to become a priest. When Clayton asked why this was, Gonville replied that he did not *want* to become a priest but knew that he had to. Clayton understood and, being a much needed father-figure, he helped Gonville through his training, both with friendship and financially, and they remained close for the rest of Clayton's life.

Soon after my meeting with Gonville something occurred which was so strange that I needed to speak to someone about it, and Gonville was there to help.

I woke in the middle of the night and heard my own voice speaking with words which had not come from my brain. I found that I was sitting up in bed and an urgent message was being passed through me to Robert, who was in bed beside me. The words were "Go immediately. The child is dying" - just that, with no explanation. Robert woke and wanted to know what on earth I had been saying. I told him that I did not know what had happened, but at that moment the words came through me again and repeated the instruction that he should go immediately to a dying child. He was obviously put out by being woken so suddenly and demanded where he was to go. I didn't know, but told him that *he* must know or the message would not have been given to him.

It so happened that Robert had been called the evening before by the parents of a child who was ill. They were not Robert's patients and he had told them that if they could not get their own doctor they were to ring again before ten o'clock. They had not rung and so he assumed that their own doctor had come. He had, however, taken down their address at the time of the call.

In view of the fact that Robert had no belief in psychic matters, it is to his credit that, after some discussion with me, he got up and went to the house. Arriving there he found that the parents had been asleep and the child quiet. The father got up to answer the door and asked who Robert was, for of course the couple had never met him. They must have been surprised that a doctor had come unbidden at three o'clock in the morning and, quite understandably, they did not want the child woken because they had had a bad time with it earlier in the night. However, Robert insisted that he must examine the child and when he did so he realised at once that it was seriously ill and in a coma. On further examination it proved to be in immediate danger with an acute strangulation of the bowel and bleeding from the rectum. He knew it was unlikely to survive the night. Alerting the emergency department at the general hospital to contact the surgeon and prepare a theatre, he put the child and the parents into his car and drove straight to the hospital. An operation was performed immediately and the child lived.

I knew nothing about the family concerned and never came in contact with them. On his return, several hours later, Robert told me what had happened, but for some reason he was absolutely adamant that I should not discuss the event with anyone. However, it was obvious that I had to talk to someone. Only I knew how strange the message had been and the means of its delivery through me, and I felt a great need to discuss it. It could not have arisen through telepathy from the parents for they were asleep and had not been roused, as the child was quiet. The only explanation I can give is that the message had come from some relative in another world, who had realised that without help the child would be dead by the morning. That my voice could be used to alert Robert in such a peremptory manner, and that he knew where the child might be, made it possible to save the child's life. As my own voice was used to deliver the message, I was unable to begin to imagine the identity of the Being who had called on us for help. The synchronicity of the situation was unusual, for to find a psychic woman (me) in bed with her husband (Robert) who was a doctor and who knew the whereabouts of the child, was certainly a rare combination! I suspect that some Being, somewhere, had worked hard through the night to save the life of the child, and, having failed to persuade the parents to wake and take it to hospital, had tried to find another way.

This was the second child whose life had been saved by an unknown source and the second time I had been used as an instrument to prevent deaths which would otherwise have been certain. Meeting Gonville had come just at the right time, however, and I was able to discuss the whole matter with him. Unlike other priests of the church, some of whom had, in the past, instructed me to have nothing to do with psychic events, he took the matter seriously and from that time onwards was of the greatest help to me in spiritual and psychic matters. I believe that a teacher always comes when the time is right, but I could never have anticipated the strength of the help which I was to find in

Gonville throughout the coming years.

Soon after I this I was in hospital, having undergone a gall-bladder operation. In those days the operation was pretty invasive and left one with serious pain. Gonville visited me in the the evenings when the wards were quiet and there were no other visitors. He was permitted this licence because it was a Roman Catholic Hospital and he was a priest, so his status impressed the nuns. One evening I told him about a dream which I had had the night before in the hospital. It was a short, vivid, disturbing dream and I believed that it was important.

In the dream I had found myself standing on the extreme edge of a massive cliff in front of which was a deep ravine. At the bottom of the ravine was a raging inferno, somewhat like a volcano at the point of eruption. Through the smoke I saw, on the far side of the ravine, a golden land to which I was being called. There was only one way to respond to the call and that was to discard all fear and leap. Then I would find myself safely on the other side. But I could not discard my fear and, without faith, I believed that I would fall into the flames. I woke from the dream filled with sorrow that I had failed the test.

Gonville did not respond to this dream with the same feelings as I had. He saw it as a blessing, a foretaste of experiences yet to come, a promise that the 'golden land' was there, even if the way to it was hard and my faith, at present, was not strong enough to make the crossing.

As I write this account of my early meetings with Gonville, I am struck by the realisation of how little I knew at that time what an important part his friendship would mean to me in the future. From this time until the end of his life, a love grew between us which has enabled me to reach a deep understanding of the misused word, 'love'.

Chapter 20

Political Awareness

In September 1956 Peter, our eldest child, went to boarding school at Peterhouse in Marandellas, about fifty miles from Salisbury. I was not happy at the idea of any of the children boarding away from home. It had always seemed to me that when you have a good home it is not necessary to send children away. The reader may question the security of our home when relations between Robert and myself were so insecure, but I have to make it clear that the children were totally unaware of the problem.

Peter was very homesick at Peterhouse and both he and I found the situation traumatic. Sally was a day-girl and was able to ride her bicycle to Arundel School, and I only had to drive the younger boys to St John's Preparatory School in Highlands, to the north of Salisbury. My days were easier, and as the Cathedral needed financial help with the extension of the building, I became involved with various projects for raising money.

Through working for the Cathedral I came to know Gonville ffrench-Beytagh as a close friend as well as a priest, and he was a great joy. I would not say that he was always the wisest person on matters political, and this was to land him in serious trouble in the future, but who am I to speak when I followed the same road? He felt very strongly about things, particularly regarding 'man's inhumanity to man', and this feeling cut right across the racial barriers which were being erected by the Smith Government all over Southern Rhodesia. South Africa was being driven by its white government into *apartheid* (an Afrikaans word meaning, just as it sounds, keeping the races apart by means of different laws for the blacks and the whites) and, judging by past history, where South Africa led Southern Rhodesia's government of the time would certainly follow.

It would seem obvious that in a country like ours, where the black (African) population outnumbered the white by millions, political progress would have to be made to assuage the anger which was arising in the hearts and minds of black Rhodesians. This anger was augmented by access to radio and television which made the discrepancies between the treatment of the races more and more obvious. The Rhodesian Government under Ian Smith, however, persistently refused even to contemplate the limited progress demanded by the African population. Both the government of the time and many of the white Rhodesian electorate were attracted by the idea of apartheid. To them the total separation of the races seemed the right solution, but to the thinking liberal element in Rhodesia this amounted to the political equivalent of putting one's head in the sand.

Amongst the educated black population a very dangerous situation was fermenting, to which the majority of white Rhodesians were oblivious. For the most part, the white people knew only their black servants, who were delightful willing people and who would certainly not get into political discussions with their employers. If asked for their opinion, which was rare, the majority would say what they thought 'the Boss' required of them. It amazed me how few of the white people known to me had ever had a serious conversation with a black Rhodesian, or knew any of their fellow black Rhodesians as friends. This state of affairs was eventually to lead to disaster.

Looking back, I realise that an incident which had occurred during my first year in Rhodesia had made a deep impression on me and may well have been the deciding factor when I became involved in politics in 1965. I had been walking down one of the main streets in Salisbury, when a middle-aged man walking ahead of me yelled "Walk in the gutter, kaffir!" and hit a small black boy across the shins with a heavy stick. The boy, who was about ten years old, was walking on the edge of the pavement. He was terrified and jumped into the gutter. I stopped him and asked if he was all right. The man, who looked like a farmer, started shouting at me, and the small boy ran away. The fact that the child was wearing a white uniform and carrying a shopping basket, suggested that he had been on an errand for his employer, and in any case the boy had every right to be where he was. The man called me a "bloody immigrant" and said it was time I learned how to treat the 'kaffirs', as "this is how we treat them in this country."

When I said that I would report him to the police, he said, "OK, lady. Take me to the police station, then." To his surprise, I did.

When we arrived at the police station I told the officer in charge that I wanted to bring an action against this man for hitting a child in the street. The policeman seemed interested until the man said that it was only a 'bloody kaffir'. The officer then asked where the child was and I had to say that he had run away. After noting down the complaint, the officer said that without the child there was no more that I could do, and that he would speak to the man and I had better go. I left, feeling sure that the policeman would do nothing, but hoping that I had shaken the man, or had at least shown him that not everyone agreed with him that a child could be hit for walking on the pavement. Before leaving I said to the man, "It is people like you who will bring war to this country one of these days." When I discussed this with Robert he felt that I should not get involved in things like that, but he had a lot to learn about me if he thought that, for one moment, I could stand by and do nothing in such a situation.

Chapter 21

The Birth of Clare

As time went on I became more and more unhappy at the state of our marriage. It had been deteriorating since my arrival in Rhodesia and recently I had written to my father asking for money to bring the children home to England. He replied asking, quite sensibly, how I proposed to live if I returned. I had hoped that he might help me, but that was obviously out of the question. My father believed that it was up to him to deal equally with all his five children, whatever their individual situation, and he could not have taken on the care of just one daughter, who had four children, when there were four other children of his own to be considered.

Gonville had no doubt that it was right for me to stay and deal with our marriage situation to the best of my ability. However, I was not good at looking the other way and Robert's behaviour was distressing me. He seemed to be absent and unavailable very often now, and I had known for a long while that there were other women in his life. I had been ill frequently over recent years, most of my problems having been caused by tension. I thought that one solution would be to have another child; I was forty-two and looked forward to caring for a new baby, as the older children were now all at school.

When eventually I told Robert that I was four months pregnant, he was shocked. It seemed that in spite of the fact that we were still sleeping together, he had not considered such a possibility. Unknown to me, at that time he had other plans for the rest of his life. However, the baby was a fact and there was no way round it and I was delighted at the prospect. Many years later my suspicions at the time were confirmed: he had met someone else at that period and had been prepared to leave us. Whether he really would have gone I do not know, but little Clare's arrival a few months later saved the situation.

The day Clare was born, Peter and Richard were getting ready to go back to boarding school. I was packing their trunks when I suddenly realised that the baby was on the way and was not going to wait for anyone. I sent all the children off to their friends and quickly made up the bed in the spare-room. I rang Robert at the surgery and asked him to alert my doctor urgently, and also to call the nurse and the physiotherapist, who was to help me with 'painless' childbirth.

Time passed and the pains increased. I rang the consulting rooms again and spoke to the sister. It turned out that Robert had not alerted any of them, because he did not believe that I could be nearly at the point of delivery. I told the sister that my contractions were coming every three minutes and that I was afraid that I was going to have the baby alone in the house. I then rang the nurse and the physiotherapist, who both turned up at once. Soon after this there was a rush of cars up Mount Pleasant Drive. The doctor and Robert arrived together and within moments Clare arrived as well. As she was a fifth child she had not waited around, but had arrived exactly when expected. I had had enough experience of labour to recognise the signs!

Robert and the children came into the room shortly after her birth and the two older boys were delighted that Clare had come just before they had to leave to return to boarding school. She was a very beautiful baby and as I had had no painkillers or any other medication she was very wide awake. She looked around the room as though she were checking out her new home.

Having a baby at home is a completely different experience from having a hospital delivery. There is a much greater sense of peace, and this was true of Clare's birth in spite of the last-minute rush on this occasion. It was also rewarding to have the children there within minutes of her birth, even before she was tidied up and washed. Clare instantly became part of the family.

Chapter 22

The Shearly Cripps
African Children's Home

More and more black Rhodesians were coming into the towns from the farming areas, and because many women had broken away from their tribes when they left the reserves, the old tradition by which orphans were taken in by relatives was dying out. The Bishop of Mashonaland realised that there was a real need for a children's home for orphaned infants and young children and those abandoned or left to fend for themselves because of the imprisonment of their mothers. Gonville ffrench-Beytagh responded to the problem by recommending me as a person likely to take on the work of founding an Anglican Church orphanage for such children! I was called to see the bishop, who outlined what he had in mind and told me that a Home could be built on mission land at Arcturus, north of Salisbury.

The St. John's Mission in Arcturus, where it was proposed to build the Home, was in a native reserve, quite a long way from the city of Salisbury, for it was much cheaper to build out there and there were no building restrictions. Building and running the Home from Salisbury, however, was not going to be easy. The bishop said that the design and finance would be up to me but that unfortunately the diocese had no money for the building! This was rather a frightening prospect, as I had no experience of raising money, understanding the requirements of an orphanage, designing one or running it once built.

An enormous amount of research was needed to discover how such a project could be undertaken. The government had to be approached and after a lot of negotiation it was agreed that the government would give pound for pound if I managed to raise the first seven thousand pounds.

Nowadays that does not sound a very large amount of money to raise, but in 1960 in Rhodesia it was a great deal to collect for an African charity. I discovered that none of the big charities would give anything until the project was under way. The Beit Trust would be generous, but only when we reached the point of laying bricks, and I had similar responses elsewhere. I was at a loss as to know how to take the first steps.

That seven thousand pounds was very hard to obtain. White Rhodesians, on the whole, were not keen to support purely Black charities and the African people themselves were not used to giving to charity. Few of them were wealthy, and most were very poor, more likely to be the beneficiaries of charity than the donors. I did not even have a petty cash account, so to make some money to meet that immediate need I set about designing a Christmas card, which I then had printed. I sold the cards to my friends, and the people who bought them were very generous (as the card was pretty awful) but in this way I raised the first hundred pounds. Then a miracle happened. The Capricorn Africa Society heard about us and offered to insert an appeal leaflet for the Home in their Christmas magazine, which circulated to members both locally and in Britain.

They wanted an appealing photo of an African child to put in the leaflet, so I took a photographer into the Salisbury township of Harare and visited the hospital, where we got a beautiful picture of a small child who, tragically, had been damaged by a petrol bomb during the riots which were going on at the time. I wanted to draw attention to the violent problems which were being experienced in Rhodesia and the leaflet also asked for financial help towards the building of the Home.

The boy's face was untouched by the explosion, but his head was bandaged and he had enormous appealing eyes. The leaflet, when distributed by Capricorn Africa in Britain, brought in several thousand pounds. I decided that it was time to form a committee and, with the aid of some very energetic women friends, I soon had constructive ideas for further fundraising. The best of these was to bring out a yearly diary containing useful recipes contributed by as many well-known people as we could find. This worked so well that forty years later it is still one of the Home's best money-raisers. The Diary continues and I noticed that the last one I received had more down-to-earth recipes than the earlier ones, so it will be of use to many more people.

Plans for the building were drawn up by a generous architect. They were as simple as it was possible to make them, but they were adequate and, built on those lines, the Home would be easy to run. By then we had raised the required seven thousand pounds and the government came up with its contribution of a further seven thousand, which enabled us to put down the foundations of the Shearly Cripps African Children's Home, and to call in the help of those charities which would now contribute towards the structure of the building.

The bishop chose the name for the Home to commemorate the work of Arthur Shearly Cripps, who had been a dearly loved priest in Rhodesia; he was a missionary poet who was closely related to the Cripps family in Britain. He had travelled on foot around the reserves caring for those African families most in need. His parishioners frequently supplied him with clothes for himself as well as for the needy, but he always returned from his expeditions in rags, having given away nearly all his own garments.

As the building progressed so did my size, for I had become pregnant with Clare at about the time that we started the project. However my pregnancy could not stand in the way of supervising the progress of the Home and I travelled the strip roads and the dusty miles to the mission several times a week. Clare was born when the project was about halfway through and after that she had to come with me. By now we had raised twenty-three thousand pounds and the end of building was in sight, and as soon as there was a roof over their heads and water laid on, the first African children came in. I was thrilled to hear their shouts of joy as they rushed up and down the concrete passages and claimed their bunk beds.

There was still much to be done, however. Water had been one of the hardest things to organise. We obtained only a meagre supply from a nearby stream and a borehole was obviously going to be one of our biggest expenses. The priest in charge of the mission was very helpful with the running of the Home, and our first Home Mother was excellent but she could not stay long. We needed to employ an African couple to live in and look after the children. We interviewed several couples, but if the wife was good the husband usually drank, or if the husband seemed just right the wife was often useless. Finally we took on a charming woman with a rather unlikely husband and hoped for the best.

Some members of my committee were shocked to find that most of the little boys got into bed with each other rather than sleeping alone! It was felt that they should be taught that it was not the thing to do, but I could see no harm in it. None of us knew what deprived backgrounds the children had come from. Most of them had been alone in the world, having lost everything, and they needed comfort. This was one harmless way in which they found it.

It was not long before things started to go wrong. Essentials like cutlery and bedding seemed to be in short supply, and before Christmas I discovered that all the presents sent to the children had disappeared. On further investigation we found that cleaning materials, lavatory paper and many other things had also gone missing. We could no longer ignore what was happening, but the question was how to find out where to place the blame. One day a member of the Committee and I were driving out to look into the matter when we noticed a white line down the side of the *kopje* - the small hill, close to the Mission. This was so odd that we stopped the car to investigate. We found a toilet roll had rolled from the top of the hill to the bottom leaving a clear path up to a cache where most of the stolen goods were hidden. God certainly does move in mysterious ways, but I doubt if He has ever used a toilet roll before.

There was little doubt that, as we had suspected, we would have to charge the Home Mother's husband with the thefts, but after consultation with the bishop we found that the Church thought otherwise. The bishop felt that prosecution would give the Church a bad name. However, I thought that we would be the laughing stock of the neighbourhood if we took no action and that nothing would be safe in future. Eventually the husband admitted that he had taken the things, and nearly everything was returned, but I felt that he had to go. This meant that we lost our excellent Home Mother as well. Finally, after many failures, we were blessed with a really able woman who had the good of the Home at heart.

There were a number of occasions when children became ill and I was called out to an emergency. I never knew what I would find because the message over the phone, having come through various sources, was often hard to understand, but I knew that I would not have been called unless things were serious. We kept a supply of ordinary medicines in the Home but these were very limited. Any child who was really ill had to be taken to the Harare Hospital in Salisbury. The worst calls came in the night and so I sometimes had to make the long journey in the dark.

One such call was to a child having fits who turned out to have a tumour on the brain. I had to drive alone with him to the hospital and leave him there. Another call was to a dying two-year-old who had whooping cough. He was one of my special children, as he was the baby of the Home. He had come to us in a bad state and we had made him well again, so it was a disaster when I found, on arriving in the night, that he was dead. A ring of chanting women sat round him with candles burning on the mud floor. I could do nothing but tell them that I would return the next day with a coffin, and that they must try to arrange for a grave to be dug.

The following day I found my way to a coffin-maker in the Harare Township and bought a sad little coffin made of orange-box wood, which I was assured was the right thing for a tiny child. It was lined with shiny pink satin and had a cheap tin crucifix nailed to the lid. Screws were supplied with which to close it. The women at the Mission thought it was wonderful. We wrapped the baby in a cloth and I screwed down the lid. No such things as death certificates were available, for there was no doctor within many miles of the Home. I had to rely on the fact that rigor mortis had set in to confirm the death, but even then I would have been thankful for another opinion before we buried the child.

There was great difficulty in digging the grave, because it was the end of the dry season and the ground was like concrete. We borrowed a pickaxe from the mission and eventually managed to dig deep enough to cover the coffin with about eighteen inches of soil. The mission priest held a short service for the burial and would, I hoped, have confirmed the death of the child through whooping-cough had there been any questions raised in the future.

Although most children who were admitted to the Home were declared at the time to have no relatives, or were perhaps children of prostitutes in prisons or mental homes, when a child died spurious relatives popped up everywhere protesting that we were to blame and that they wanted compensation. Our usual reply was to tell them, firstly, that they would have to prove their relation to the child in question and, secondly, that they would have to pay for the upkeep of the child for the time it had been in the Home. They usually disappeared at once.

We came upon another unexpected problem when African mothers, who were pillars of the Anglican Church, expected us to take in their children while they had a holiday. They could not understand why the child of a prostitute should be taken into what they considered to be the luxury of the Home, while they, who went to church every Sunday, could not benefit from a Home owned by their church. As time progressed the members of the African Mother's Union became our loyal supporters and were helpful in explaining to the local African population the way in which the Home had to be run.

It was at this time that Gonville sent a message asking me to come down and meet him in the Cathedral. I wondered whether he was going to land me with another project. When I found him in the cloisters we sat down on a bench and he took my hand and said, "I have something to tell you and I don't want you to hear it from anyone else." I felt a cold hand on my heart in anticipation of what he was going to say. He told me that he had been offered the post of Dean of the Cathedral in Johannesburg and that he had decided to accept it. This meant that he would be leaving shortly. I was shattered, for it was through his constant support that I had managed to keep my family together through the previous ten years. I told him that I did not know how I would be able to go on without him. He assured me that I would and that I was strong, but at that moment I was anything but strong and could hardly restrain the tears which threatened to overwhelm me. We sat for a while in the peace of the cloister garden and then he got up to go, and as we left he took my hand, saying "You will always be my pearl of great price."

Death by drought of a child in Africa

In the kia, mothers moaning,
chanting, ululating low,
sitting cross-legged on the dust floor
women only, men no go.

Little child is lying slackly,
in the candle-light he seems
far from home and never moving,
carried to the land of dreams.

No-one's baby, two years lonely,
homeless, he came here to die.
Watching him the mothers mourn him
hear his last, thin, wailing cry.

I from city bring the coffin,
orange-box lined pink inside,
close beside it lies the cover
nailed with tin Christ crucified.

Little baby cannot hear me
using hammer for the nailing,
closing lid upon his beauty
to the chanting women's wailing.

Come the men with pick and shovel,
digging through the dried up crust.
Africa has space for millions
Under arid, stricken dust.

Chapter 23

The Formation of the Centre Group

For some years before I left Rhodesia the political situation had become increasingly difficult. The Committee running the Shearly Cripps Home was extremely efficient and had relieved me from sole responsibility, freeing me to add my weight to the small group of white people who were battling to support the cause of the black Rhodesians in their requests for advancement.

The Centre Group was a liberal pressure group which various young men and I had formed at the time when, following the example of South Africa, Ian Smith's government was demonstrating its extreme racial policies. We had formed the group because of our common opposition to the growing evidence of the inhumanity shown by the policies of the Rhodesia Front Party, which now governed the country. Winston Field, the previous Prime Minister, had been pressured into resigning, and the Rhodesia Front had put Ian Smith in his place. To those of us who were trying to keep our finger on the pulse of the government, the possibility of Rhodesian UDI (Unilateral Declaration of Independence from Britain) was seen to be a very real threat.

Sir Anthony Nutting had come from Britain to assess the situation and we, the Centre Group, approached him for advice on the advisability of launching as a political party. He recommended that we should maintain our stand as a pressure group for as long as we could, rather than embarking on a change. We took his advice and continued to tour the country, hoping to open the eyes of white Rhodesians to the ever-present dangers of following South Africa into a policy of apartheid, and of the resultant racial violence which would inevitably follow.

The reason why the Rhodesia Front (the RF) under Ian Smith was determined on UDI arose from Smith's abortive discussions with the British Government. It had been made plain over and over again that Britain would not tolerate apartheid in Rhodesia. Ian Smith, however, religiously followed the thinking of the South African government and was determined to cut Rhodesia's ties with Britain in order to govern Rhodesia as he thought fit. It was apparent to the members of the Centre Group that the making of UDI and the imposing of apartheid on the people would, almost certainly, result in a racial war, and we did our best to educate the country into political awareness of the threat to peace. As a pressure group we held meetings with both black and white people. We found much interest among black Rhodesians, but had violent reactions from many of the white people. Ian Smith had been built up by the white community into the likeness of a saviour of his country, and party-political blindness had obscured the vision of the majority of white Rhodesians.

Sir Humphrey Gibbs had the unenviable task of being Governor of Rhodesia during this period. As he and Lady Gibbs held out in Government House the situation became tense. There was a very real threat to Sir Humphrey himself, whose presence prevented the Rhodesia Front from making a declaration of independence from Great Britain. Sir Humphrey, a Privy Councillor, held his post as Governor by command of the Queen, and there was no way in which he could have agreed to a declaration of rebellion against her.

Legally, Ian Smith needed to declare a State of Emergency if he was to carry out his plans for the country, and he needed the signature of the Governor to authenticate such a declaration. After assurances to the Governor (first from the Chief of Police that a state of emergency was essential owing to the growing violence in the country, and then from Ian Smith that it was needed on security grounds only, and not for political purposes) Sir Humphrey was persuaded to sign the required document. As part of his assurance Smith guaranteed categorically that he would not use the State of Emergency in order to make a Unilateral Declaration of Independence.

Within days, while Sir Hugh Beadle (the Chief Justice) was out of the country having consultations with the British Prime Minister, Harold Wilson, Ian Smith broke his word, declaring independence beneath a portrait of the Queen. He made this move maintaining all the while that Rhodesia remained totally loyal to Her Majesty! Later it was discovered that the original Declaration had been signed undated and was therefore invalid. Whether this had been done intentionally or through incompetence is not known.

Sir Humphrey and Lady Gibbs and Sir Hugh Beadle, who, on his return from Britain had taken up residence with the Governor in Government House, became self-imposed prisoners there, together with others who were on the staff. The danger was that if the Governor left Government House he would be prevented from returning and the new self-styled President, Clifford Dupont, would be installed.

Sir Humphrey now found himself pushed into the impossible position of having to decide whether to declare Smith's government illegal or not, in the face of the ever-present possibility of precipitating violence amongst Rhodesia's armed forces as well as between black and white Rhodesians. He also knew that once Government House had been taken over by a President, he, as a deposed Governor, might even have to leave the country. This was unthinkable without permission from the Queen herself. He would also be handing over the country to a right-wing group which intended to enforce apartheid against the wishes of the British Parliament.

Over the following days many of us lined our cars across the entrances to Government House in an attempt to prevent the police from entering and arresting the Governor. We could not have stopped them, but our action would have forced them to commit such an action openly and under protest, rather than in secret. Legally, only the Press were permitted to collect in the street in this way and we had to pose as journalists. I stood my ground as a reporter with notebook and pencil, but probably fooled no-one for long. Intense pressure to resign was put upon the Governor by Smith, Clifford Dupont and Lardner Burke, the Minister of Law and Order, but Sir Humphrey stood firm.

Interminable discussions began between the Rhodesian and British Governments and after some negotiation (and, presumably, after assurances for the safety of his position) Sir Humphrey Gibbs was used as a go-between, as he was the only legal representative of the country. Within parts of Rhodesia racial violence increased to the level of civil war. In January 1968 newspapers were censored and appeared on the streets with blank columns where the Government Censor, a man called P. K. Van der Byl, had removed articles overnight. Soon after this we in the Centre Group began publishing *Centre Point*, the monthly political newspaper of what was to become the Centre Party and, as editor, I was in serious danger of being arrested because of the articles it contained. It was illegal to publish anything which might cause 'alarm and despondency' and that meant a complete clamp-down on any opinions other than those held by the Rhodesia Front. The opinions of Sir Roy Welensky and Lord Malvern were censored out with the rest, even although these were two of Rhodesia's 'grand old men' of politics, who with the original Rhodesia Party (the RP) had been in government before the formation of the RF.

The fact that RF policies were themselves causing 'alarm and despondency' among vast numbers of black and many white Rhodesians was ignored by the government. The *Rhodesia Herald* newspaper was so severely censored that on more than one occasion it appeared with an almost completely blank front page. A ludicrous situation arose when, to try to disguise the fact that their was any dissension against government policy, and to prevent the publication of such articles in a newspaper, P. K. Van der Byl attempted to bring in a Bill forbidding any newspaper from publishing with white spaces: all articles removed by the censor during the night had to be replaced with something else before the morning. The editor of the *Rhodesia Herald* courageously decided to ignore this. He claimed that it was quite impossible to publish a newspaper without any white spaces between articles or around the edges of the pages. The government was made to look foolish and the

Bill banning white spaces was rapidly dropped. I have many letters sent to me by the editor of the *Herald* apologising for the white space on a particular page where a letter or an article by me had been removed by censorship.

In 1970 Sir Humphrey found his position had become untenable and, with permission from the Queen, he resigned as Governor of Rhodesia.

Chapter 24

The First Election
in the Rhodesian Republic

When negotiations between the Rhodesian and British Governments came to an end and Rhodesia became a republic, Smith decided to go to the country and declared a date for a general election. He wanted to have the country's approval for the policies his party was following, because he had reached his present position as Prime Minister through devious means, forcing out his predecessor and taking control of the government without the consent of the country.

It was at this point that the Centre Group immediately became the Centre Party. It was formed by the more liberal thinkers in Rhodesia, although sadly there had been a split between them and the old Rhodesia Party (the RP), which had become stuck in a middle-of-the-road policy. The RP would not go the whole way towards the political demands of the African people, as it considered the idea of having mixed-race schools and black members in parliament was going too far! The Centre Party believed that it was imperative to meet at least some of the demands of the African people in order to overcome the racism of the diehard Whites. They considered it equally important to widen the vision of those who maintained the historical 'paternalistic' approach to black Africa, and these attitudes angered the RP.

P. K. Van der Byl stormed into the fray saying that white farmers would rather burn their farms than allow black people the right to own any of the farming land (all of which, apart from the African Reserves, was in the hands of white people until this point). Ian Smith also stated that equal voting rights with black Africans would happen 'over my dead body' and 'not in a thousand years'. We in the Centre Party saw this as political suicide (and by the end of the century, judging by the violent recriminations being perpetrated in Zimbabwe, we were proved right).

The Centre Party put up candidates for the eight black seats which the Government eventually permitted in Parliament, and I firmly believe that had the Government consulted with black Rhodesians at this time, and shown that it was willing to meet many of their needs, a peaceful transition might even then have been achieved and we might well have prevented the bloody war which finally blighted the country. Such a change in attitude came to pass years later in South Africa when events were influenced by the disaster which occurred in Rhodesia. The South Africans amended their policies and so far have avoided a civil war. Personally, I hold Ian Smith and his advisors responsible for much of the disaster of present-day Zimbabwe. It is more than possible that a different attitude on the part of the Government at that time would have enabled the country to have changed peacefully. The refusal to make any move towards the needs of the African people, gave them no way forward except by violence.

In Rhodesia the multi-racial Centre Party prepared to fight the election in every constituency. This meant that everyone had to pull his or her weight. Pat Bashford, a Rhodesian tobacco farmer, had bravely agreed to 'stick his neck out' and become President of the Party. He was supported by a committee of extremely able, wise and energetic younger men and women (including Nic McNally, who for many years, even during the growing turmoil in what is now Zimbabwe, retained his seat in parliament). We knew that fighting every constituency was a gesture that we were making and that the most we could hope for was a seat or two on the White benches in parliament, but we had great hopes of winning all the eight Black seats which had, at last, been permitted in the House by the government. However, eight seats for black people in a country the size of France, while the white people were entitled to sixty, was hardly a convincing ratio. The Centre Party was the only Party which had the courage to hold political meetings in the Reserves (black areas) or in the townships (black towns).

I recall a Rhodesia Front meeting held in Mount Pleasant, Salisbury, near to the University, addressed by Ian Smith. The Centre Party turned out in some numbers, as did the supporters of the Rhodesia Front, and many black and white Rhodesian students from the University filled one half of the hall. The opening speech by the RF was extremely provocative, with no attempt being made to consider the feelings of the black audience. When the Prime Minister got up to speak and launched into the Government's policy of apartheid, an undercurrent of humming could be heard coming from the area of the hall in which the University students were seated. It soon grew to such a pitch that it was impossible to hear the Prime Minister's words. RF supporters went outside and turned on hoses through the windows, soaking the Africans in the hall, and the police entered in force. It was clear that the Front had called on the police in advance, realising that there was likely to be trouble. The black students rose and made their way slowly out of the hall, singing *Sikelele Afrika* (God Save Africa) as they went. Their pace was as that of the chameleon, two steps forward and one back.

The Prime Minister danced triumphantly on the platform with the microphone in his hands, singing a South African rugby song in Afrikaans which, roughly translated, meant "Baboons get back up the mountain." It was lucky for all of us that the students did not appear to know Afrikaans, or there could have been a riot. The members of the Rhodesia Front, who filled the seats below the platform, rose and cheered, and the Prime Minister acknowledged their approval with glee. Members of the Centre Party and other liberal Rhodesians who were present were shocked to see a Prime Minister sink to such levels.

Being extremely angry, I rose and demanded whether Mr Smith considered himself to be Prime Minister of all Rhodesians, black and white. Did he not feel that his behaviour was pushing the country towards a situation similar to that which pertained in France at the time of the French Revolution, when so-called aristocrats refused to listen to the masses of underprivileged people? The Prime Minister laughed derisively, and replied "Ah down't speak Frinch, but the answer is NONG.'

Applause rang out from his devoted supporters, but we others followed the black students out of the Hall, many of us in tears at the realisation that, under Smith, there was no hope for Rhodesia as a united country in the future.

Centre Party public meetings were always attended by the police and were heckled violently by hard-line RF supporters. Eggs were thrown and attempts were made to shout the speakers down, but Pat Bashford seemed to enjoy it and remained calm. The situation was frequently saved by his wonderful sense of humour and his ability to cool potentially inflammatory remarks. The presence of the police was, of course, far more threatening to the black members of the Party than it was to the white members, something of which we were all aware. It was very much easier for the police to arrest a black person than a white, for the arrest of white people usually hit international headlines, whereas black people could disappear without trace.

In the end the election results gave the Centre Party all eight Black seats in the House, but only 23% of the White vote and no White seats. When the elected black members of the House took their seats, the manners of the Rhodesia Front towards them were appalling, and in the face of such behaviour the patience shown by the African members of the opposition astounded us.

No allowance was made by the government members for the fact that English was not the mother-tongue of the black members, and that they suffered, on the whole, from having been allowed little education. I recall the elected Leader of the Opposition, Micah Bhebe, coming to me with a copy of his maiden speech and asking me to check it over before he made it in the House. I suggested that he should read it to me. He began by saying "Mr Prime Minister and gentlemen, it is my wish that we should all work together towards peace in this country and for that purpose I will put my spanner in the works." At this I had to stop him and point out that this idiom did not mean what he thought it did. I tried to explain the real meaning, but he was indignant. He was rather proud of using the phrase and insisted that he "only wanted to tighten up the bolts". Finally, however, I managed to convince him that it would not be wise to use it in this context. Had he not had the sense to come to me for advice he would have been jeered at and ridiculed in the House and would not have known the reason why.

The results of the Election proved to the African people that roughly a quarter of the white voters were prepared to agree to changes in favour of black needs in the running of the country, but the proportion of black members permitted in the House held out no hope to black Rhodesians that the changes they wanted could be achieved through parliament. We had at least got eight Black seats in the House, all of them now under the umbrella of the Centre Party, but the ridicule which continued to be suffered by the eight black members from the overwhelming number of the white members on the Government benches, was scandalous to say the least. When reported in Hansard, it deepened the rifts between the races. On many occasions I heard Opposition speakers in the House interrupted by cries of "Cut your tail off and get back up a tree!" along with other offensive and inflammatory remarks.

The Centre Party had done its best to persuade the white people that the only hope of avoiding civil war was to meet at least some of the needs of the black people, but we had failed. There had never been much chance that we would succeed, but in forming a multi-racial Party we had hoped that we would stir up all the right-minded people of the country to do something to prevent the evil of war. The basis upon which we had formed our belief had been Edmund Burke's well-known observation, "All that is necessary for the triumph of evil is that good men do nothing."

Chapter 25

My Part in Rhodesian Politics

From the time that the Centre Group was launched in the mid 1960's until 1972 when my family and I left Africa for good, my actions had put us all under considerable strain. Robert was in a difficult position, for most of the old Fynn family friends were racially minded and did not approve of the Centre Party. My letters to the newspaper - those which managed to get past the censor - upset them, and they were inclined to write to Robert and tell him to keep his wife under control. He also had his medical practice to consider. I was convinced, on the other hand, that if we were to save the country from a full-scale war we had to expose the foolishness of the Smith Government's policy of apartheid. We had three sons who were within the call-up age and they had no wish to fight their black friends.

We knew that, as a family, we were *persona non grata* with the Police. We had discovered that our telephone was tapped when, one Monday morning, my eldest son Peter picked up the receiver and heard a message, recorded by Robert the previous weekend, saying that he was not on duty. Peter realised that this was strange: the message should not have been relayed to us but only to incoming callers. He replaced the receiver and checked the answerphone, but found it turned off. By the time we tried the line again the telephone-tapping department had realised their error and had corrected it. It seemed that some incompetent person must have left our line connected in such a way that we were able to hear the conversations the police had recorded the day before! It would not have done Robert's practice any good if his patients had learned that his phone was tapped and was no longer private.

Tellingly, the same thing happened on the Government House telephone around the same period. Also on a Monday, GH picked up a message which they had left on their phone from the previous weekend.

It was interesting to find myself on the wrong side of the law in Rhodesia, having been for so many years in MI5 in Britain, working for the government and bound by the Official Secrets Act.

A few years later Peter married a girl called Gill Boney, who was a staunch supporter of the Centre Party and accompanied me to many political meetings. I had become recognisable to many of the RF Ministers who addressed meetings and my efforts to question them were usually ignored, so Gill and I made a plan to overcome this. She would ask a question, bringing up an uncomfortable subject which the Government would prefer not to discuss, and when she was fobbed off I would then rise to my feet wearing dark glasses and sometimes a headscarf. Only when I had been allowed to put my question would I remove my disguise so that I was recognised. In this way we were able to ask the Minister of the Interior questions on the scandal of newspaper censorship of material supposedly likely to cause 'alarm and despondency' (that is, in reality, anything which questioned the government's attitude to the racial problem).

One such question revealed that a letter I had written to the *Rhodesia Herald*, in which I quoted the words of Cecil John Rhodes, had been censored. This was, of course, embarrassing to the Government, for Rhodesians looked upon Cecil Rhodes as the hero Founder of the country. The Rhodesia Front frequently quoted Rhodes themselves, but used only the first part of one of his original speeches - an extract which appeared to indicate that he felt that only the white population of Rhodesia was 'civilised'.

On this occasion, Jack Howman, then Minister of Internal Affairs, answered the question about the censoring of my letter. He told the audience that no letter of mine would have been censored if it was only putting forward the opinion of a third party. I replied that the opinion put forward in my letter was not mine but was the opinion of the founder of the country, Cecil John Rhodes, and with permission I proceeded to read aloud the censored letter:

To The Editor, *The Rhodesia Herald.*

Sir,

I quote Cecil John Rhodes:-

> *My motto is equal rights for every*
> *civilised man south of the Zambesi.....*
>
> *What is a civilised man? A man,*
> *whether white or black, who has*
> *sufficient education to write his name,*
> *has some property or works, in fact is*
> *not a loafer.*

The first part of this quotation is often repeated in Rhodesia today, the last part is virtually unknown to the average Rhodesian. Surely we have gone far enough in our failure to give Rhodes full credit for the whole of his belief?

Diana Fynn

As this was a direct quotation from Rhodes himself it was difficult for Howman to stop me. There was much anger from the platform. P. K. van der Byl, who was in charge of censorship, objected to the exchange, clearly rattled because it revealed the iniquity of the government censorship department. It had been hiding behind the myth that only material which endangered the country was excluded from the newspapers. Obviously this quotation put Rhodes' intention for the the country in a nutshell and held out hope for the future of Rhodesia. It therefore challenged the policies of the Rhodesia Front Party, rather than endangered the country as a whole.

I had ended my letter to the *Rhodesia Herald* with a famous quotation from Abraham Lincoln:

> *You can fool all the people some of the time and*

some of the people all of the time, but you cannot
fool all of the people all of the time.

Writing this account - from memory, from my notes made at the time and from old copies of the *Centre Point* newspaper - has stirred up many thoughts which I had during that period. In 1946 when I first arrived in what was then Southern Rhodesia, I had been struck by the fact that many white people seemed to believe that the *status quo* with the black population would go on for ever. Sir Godfrey Huggins as Prime Minister ran a stable government as he had done for many years. The country was peaceful, the Second World War had ended and it seemed that nothing had changed or would change. However, witnessing the paternal attitude adopted by so many white Rhodesians to their black compatriots, and having come from a war-ravaged Britain myself, I saw a country trying to remain in the past, in a world which was being thrust into an unexplored future. The conservative thinkers seemed to forget that black Rhodesians had served in the forces throughout the war and had travelled and seen the world in a new light.

Prime Minister Sir Godfrey Huggins, who has already been mentioned in this book as the doctor whose medical practice Robert joined in 1946, was a wise and forward-looking man. Since the war, he had realised that changes would have to occur and that it was not possible to maintain white supremacy indefinitely, but unfortunately he himself could not remain Prime Minister for ever. Big changes were taking place in the neighbouring countries of Northern Rhodesia and Nyasaland. In 1953 a Federation of these two countries with our country, Southern Rhodesia, had been set up by the British. However there was little hope that this would work in view of the different forms of government in each of the three countries. After the failure of Federation in 1963, Northern Rhodesia became Zambia, Nyasaland took the name of Malawi and Southern Rhodesia reverted to plain Rhodesia, the name originally given to the whole region in honour of Cecil John Rhodes.

As time went on the Rhodesia Front Party led by Winston Field formed the Government. Winston was more open minded than the rest of his party, which demanded that South African right-wing policies should be adopted as the only way to preserve white control. Field was ousted and Smith, the leader of the right wing within the party, took over. Racism was firmly established and apartheid was the next step unless something drastic was to happen. The drastic events which *did* happen, caused by the threat of apartheid, were inevitable, leading to violence and thence to all-out civil war. Politics is the "art of the possible", but the Rhodesia Front never learned this.

It may seem strange to see a similarity between these events and the problems facing us in Britain today, but many people in Britain fail to recognise the fact that the Empire no longer exists, and cannot see that the bread spread upon its waters in the past can no longer be ignored when it comes back as a tide of immigrants into Britain. Rhodesia failed to go with its own tide, refusing to admit the needs of the majority of its people, both to be educated and to be treated as equals, and the result was tragic. Britain's situation is, of course, different in many ways, but until we all realise that the past has gone, that the loss of the Empire means that we have become just another part of a world which demands equality, and that the 'good old days' of the past were achieved by our domination of less privileged peoples, we cannot hope to play our part in the promotion of peace. Over many years Britain gave protection to millions in different parts of the world, and now we see the results. Britain is looked on as a haven for the oppressed and we should be proud that this is so.

These thoughts have arisen after watching the downfall of a prosperous country through the lack of vision of an elected party which could not see the results of its racial policies. All who knew the old Rhodesia can only mourn its loss, but must be aware that this came about by the refusal on the part of the Government to acknowledge the needs of **all** its people and to listen to the very reasonable requests of the black Rhodesians at a time when much could have been done to solve many problems. We in the Centre Party tried our utmost to instil some common sense into Rhodesia Front politics but we met with whitewashed brick walls on all sides.

It grieved Sir Godfrey Huggins (who by then had assumed the title of Lord Malvern) to have to watch his beloved country being systematically destroyed by an inept government consisting of racially biased men. He had been a wise leader of the country for many years and was revered by both black and white Rhodesians.

The Funeral of Lord Malvern

When Sir Humphrey Gibbs, after prolonged efforts on behalf of the Queen, had been forced out of his position as Governor, Clifford Dupont had been installed by Smith as President. Lord Malvern died soon after this and his funeral took place in Salisbury Cathedral, which was filled to capacity. Members of the government and their followers filled the whole of the left-hand side of the nave with Smith and Dupont and other members of the Cabinet in the front seats. Lady Malvern and her family sat in the front pew on the right of the aisle and their African servants sat in the pew behind them. In the third pew were Sir Humphrey and Lady Gibbs and their ADC. Robert and I were with them because Robert was to read the lesson. Behind us the seats were taken by Pat Bashford, leader of the Centre Party, many other members of the party, those who had supported Gibbs as Governor, and a great many of the Malverns' friends. An unusual political situation had arisen by which the Left were on the right and the Right were on the left!

Before the service began Dupont's ADC approached the servants seated behind the Malvern family, and told them to go to the back of the church. The Africans were distressed because they did not know what to do. The Malvern family was incensed and so was Sir Humphrey Gibbs in the pew behind them, who leant forward and told them to stay sitting where they were. The bishop, seeing what was happening, came up from the main door where he was waiting to escort the coffin into the

Cathedral and told the servants to stay seated, saying very firmly and audibly "The Cathedral is the House of God and not a Government building." He then crossed the aisle and arranged for 'President' Dupont and Prime Minister Ian Smith to lead the coffin out at the end of the service. At the time this seemed like a conciliatory gesture but it turned out to be otherwise.

Lord Malvern had arranged that his coffin would be carried by medical students from the University, one of each race and colour. After the service the coffin was carried from the chancel and the bishop, the 'President', the Prime Minister and other members of the government led the procession down the aisle. The Malvern family, their servants, Sir Humphrey and Lady Gibbs and a great many who were loyal to the Queen, followed behind the coffin. At the main door the bishop directed the government party to either side of the aisle to allow the coffin to take precedence. It was followed outside by the Malvern family, their servants, the Gibbs, Pat Bashford, the Centre Party sympathisers and many of Lord Malvern's friends and supporters of the deposed Governor. In this way Sir Humphrey Gibbs left the church ahead of the usurping 'President'. Lord Malvern would have approved of this arrangement!

Lord Malvern's passing was mourned by many people of all persuasions. He had been a much loved figurehead for a great many years and his death signalled the death of the old Rhodesia.

Chapter 26

Serious Political Problems

I had no previous experience of publishing a newspaper, but there is always a first time for everything so when, towards the end of the 1960's, the Party decided that it must have some form of publication *Centre Point* was suggested and it fell to me, as Secretary of the Party, to edit it, collect articles, write for it, get it printed and arrange its circulation. It was only a monthly paper but it was quite a job. In the second edition there were two important articles, the first concerning the European Property Owners Residential (Protection) Bill and the second being the report on the inquiry into the death of Leopold Takawira, an African who had died in gaol. Both of these were highly inflammatory subjects.

The Property Owners Residential (Protection) Bill, known to the public as the POP Bill, was put before the House ostensibly to protect the rights of home owners, but was in fact a bill to prevent non-Europeans from buying property or living in 'white' areas. Under the Bill 'European' meant 'not a member of the Asian or Coloured denominations': black Rhodesians were, of course, already excluded. Thus people living at the time in European areas, whose colour was questioned by 15 residents of that area, would be called upon to establish their 'white' descent by the Investigator appointed by the Minister of Justice, or to leave the area.

The Minister of Local Government, Mr Partridge, introduced the Bill, saying that it bore no relation to the South African Group Areas Act, but this was obviously untrue. If the Bill was passed it would mean that all Coloured or Asian families already resident in so-called European Residential Areas could be forced to move out of their homes. It seemed to us that this was a direct indication of the Nazi attitude of the Rhodesia Front, and the Centre Party fought this Bill at every opportunity.

In 1971, at the time when the government was doing its best to get the Property Owner's Residential Protection Act through parliament, the Right Honourable the Minister for Law and Order, Mr Desmond Lardner-Burke, addressed a congregation gathered together in the Cathedral in Salisbury, actually speaking from the pulpit! He began his 'sermon' with the statement that Christ never preached that everyone was equal, nor did He preach that everyone was entitled to equal portions in all spheres of life. So far so good, but he went on to say:

> As I understand it, when He said 'In my Father's house are many mansions......I go to prepare a place for you', he indicated that there could never be equality and that each person should be dealt with according to his abilities and his achievements.

Mr Lardner-Burke then asked his audience:

> If there was to be equality, why would there be different mansions in his Father's house? Surely there would have been one mansion where everyone was entitled to go?

The rest of Mr Lardner-Burke's speech appeared to support the fact that God approved of separate development, the POP Bill and apartheid. He did not actually say that the mansions set aside for the use of black people would be inferior to those given to white people, but the implication was there. He added that there were Christians who were trying to impose their own ambitions on the Government, and that if this was allowed to continue there would be complete chaos.

He said:

> How many times have we heard from professed Christians that the present government is not acting within Christian principles? I deny this. Why are these statements made? Presumably because those professing these thoughts do not care if there is chaos in the country. We must have laws for

all the people, and if these laws are broken punishment must be meted out to the wrongdoer. If by removing a person from circulation we entitle other persons to live in peace [this referred to the POP Bill] then surely it is the Christian duty of the Government to remove such a person.

I quote this at length because it shows the limitations exhibited even by the Minister of Law and Order in Rhodesia at that time, when trying to justify a Bill which would enable fifteen white (i.e European) residents to object to the presence of any other residents who could not prove their white descent. This could then cause the other residents and their families to be forcibly removed from their homes. The Bill was applicable to Coloureds, Indians, Chinese people and others - but not to Japanese people, who were in a different class because Japan was contributing to Rhodesia's progress by trading with us in spite of sanctions! It is unbelievable, but in Rhodesia at that time the Japanese were considered White, while the Chinese were Black, and the great majority of white people in Rhodesia considered this to be perfectly reasonable. Ultimately the POP Act never reached the Statute Books because the Party was not capable of overcoming the enormous legal problems of designing such legislation.

In the same edition of *Centre Point* we reported on the inquiry into the death of Leopold Takawira, who had died through lack of proper care in Salisbury Gaol. I attended the inquiry as a representative of *Centre Point* and found myself one of a handful of white people amongst a large number of black people. The white doctor in charge of the gaol was cross-questioned for two hours by a lawyer named Eastwood acting on behalf of Mrs Takawira. It appeared that at no time had the doctor diagnosed diabetes, from which Mr Takawira collapsed and died a short time after he had eventually been admitted to the Harare Hospital.

One of the most effective witnesses called by Mr Eastwood was an inmate of the gaol, a small man who had been confined on the same political charges as Mr Takawira. His evidence was given in English, although the magistrate tried to insist that questions to the witness, which were translated into the Shona language, should be answered in Shona and translated into English. This would have given the court ample opportunity to tamper with the evidence given and so this witness refused to go along with it. His evidence was given in a most convincing manner, in excellent English, and showed the court that there had been serious negligence on the part of the doctor, who had never examined the patient himself, in spite of repeated requests that the patient should be allowed to go to hospital. The evidence was so damning that the doctor was removed from his post forthwith.

When I returned home I told my husband about the witness in the case who, although his appearance was marred by third-rate clothing from the gaol, had been so impressive. I had come to the conclusion that he would go far and, in my opinion, could become the next President of the country when the African majority took over, as they were bound to do eventually through sheer numbers. My husband thought I was mad and asked the name of this man, but I could only tell him that as far as I had been able to discover in court he was a little-known man whose name was Mugabe!

Chapter 27

South Africa's Reaction to my Visit

In 1969 I went down to South Africa to visit Gonville ffrench-Beytagh, now Dean of the Cathedral in Johannesburg. He was in serious danger of being arrested because of his intense dislike of apartheid and his belief in justice for black South Africans. We had dinner together in a restaurant where he had booked a table over his telephone.

Later this was shown to have been a mistake. During dinner we felt able to discuss all his political problems very frankly as we were not in his flat which he knew to be 'bugged'. My time in MI5 had given me insights into situations of this sort and I ought to have considered the possibility that we were being overheard even in this locality. There was a vase of flowers on our table and, towards the end of dinner, I realised that a single man, who had been seated in a far corner of the restaurant when we arrived, had finished his meal a long time before but had remained at his table. This disturbed me and I mentioned it to Gonville, who said that he felt it could cause him no more trouble than he was already in. After my return to Rhodesia I received evidence confirming my suspicions.

A month before this Gonville had had his car burnt out and he had been threatened in many other ways over the preceding months, but he was a courageous man and refused to change his attitude. He had been particularly distressed by an *agent provocateur* who had been planted on him by the government in an effort to persuade him to break the law. If he had done so, the authorities would then have had grounds for his arrest. This young man came to him saying that he wished to join the priesthood and needed instruction. He seemed to be a genuine Christian in sympathy with Gonville, and in private conversation the man indicated that he was against the South African Government. Gonville was completely taken in by him and gave him much of his time as he instructed him on the priesthood. As tension grew around Gonville and he was threatened again and again by the police, the young man offered to obtain a gun for him in order to defend himself if he were violently attacked.

Gonville was horrified: the idea that he should shoot his way out appalled him and he began to doubt the veracity of the man's intentions. (When Gonville was later taken to trial, the same young man turned up as a witness for the prosecution).

A short while after this Gonville was visited in his flat by plain-clothes police. They searched the flat in his presence and retrieved a shoe box full of Communist literature from the top of the wardrobe in his spare room. They demanded to know what it was and Gonville told them that it did not belong to him and that he had never seen it before. He was handed the top paper and unwisely took it and gave it back, saying again that he knew nothing about it. Of course the police later claimed that because his fingerprints were on it, it must be his! The South African Secret Police were adept at this sort of trickery. Within days Gonville was under arrest.

While in South Africa I had spoken with a woman called Helen Joseph, who was under house arrest. Helen had made it her job to visit banned African families in their Homelands. White people were forbidden to visit those who had been banned, but she bravely drove her little car miles out into the bush in order to find out how these people were managing and what their needs were. I met her in the Cathedral at a Sunday morning service in order to give her messages of support from friends in Rhodesia. She was permitted to go to church provided she only spoke to one person at a time, and I felt that I would not get her into trouble if I spoke to her on my own. However, she warned me that she was under constant observation and that it would not do *me* any good. She was right.

Two days after my return to Rhodesia I was notified by the Department of the Interior in Pretoria that my right to enter South

Africa had been suspended and that should I arrive at any port of access into the Union I would be denied entry.

The letter read as follows:

(Copy of a document sent to me by the Department of the Interior, Pretoria. Original badly faded.)

16.5.1969

Mrs Diana Flynn, *sic*
Shotover,
36 Mt Pleasant Drive,
Salisbury,
Rhodesia.

Madam,

I have to inform you that the Honourable the Minister of the Interior has under the powers vested in him by section 7 bis (3) of the Aliens Act, No. 1 of 1937, withdrawn in your case, the exemption from the provisions of section 2(b) of the Act, granted to citizens of the United Kingdom and Colonies, in terms of which they are permitted to enter and sojourn in the Republic of South Africa without being in possession of Aliens Temporary Permits.

2. Similarly, the exemption from the visa requirements as laid down in section 24(1)(c)of the Admission of Persons to the Union, Regulation Act, No.22 of 1913, as amended, has also been withdrawn in your case.

3. The withdrawal of these exemptions means that before you can enter the Republic, you must be in possession of a visa as well as an Aliens Temporary Permit.

4. Application for such a visa must be made to the nearest South African Diplomatic or Consular representative abroad or to the Secretary for the Interior, Pretoria, well in advance of any contemplated visit.

5. Should you arrive at any South African port of entry without a visa you will not be permitted to enter.

Yours faithfully,

SECRETARY FOR THE INTERIOR

When returning to England a couple of years later I needed to travel across South Africa by train because my family and I were going to make the journey by sea from the port of Capetown. I applied for a South African visa but, as expected, I was refused one! Permission was not even granted for me to over-fly the country. The original letter was, in fact, the equivalent of a banning order. I would have been interested to know which meeting had instigated this reaction: my time with Gonville or with Helen Joseph. I suspect it was a combination of both, but if I had had to guess between them I would have put my money heavily upon Gonville, as they were out to get him by any means in their power.

These meetings in South Africa, coupled perhaps with the fact that I had been employed by MI5 during the war, were sufficient to prevent me from making any further visits to the Union. Sir Robert Tredgold, who had been a great friend of my husband's father, and who had recently resigned from his position as Chief Justice of Rhodesia, came to see me shortly after my return from South Africa and congratulated me. He wondered if I recalled the man in the southern states of America who, when asked what it was like when they tarred and feathered him for befriending the black people, replied, 'T'wd have been unbearable had it not been for the honour'. However, I did not feel that I had done nearly sufficient to warrant the honour bestowed on me by the South African Government.

Chapter 28

Returning to England

In 1970 Robert and I decided that we would soon have to return to England. I had reluctantly faced the fact that there was nothing constructive that I could do and that the Centre Party was no longer viable. Towards the end of the year I left Salisbury and flew home to find a house to rent, or perhaps even to buy with help from my family. My oldest son Peter was already living in England and I was also hoping to attend the christening of our second grandson.

Moving permanently to England was not going to be easy. No savings could be taken out of Rhodesia, nor could possessions be moved abroad except on a minimal and temporary basis. The only way to leave was for Robert to take a further degree in a hospital abroad, officially to further his medical experience with a view to returning to Rhodesia. We would then be permitted to take a few basic items with us.

Alan and Rosemary Milton, at the University of Rhodesia and Nyasaland in Salisbury, were close friends of ours and Alan told me that if I had no plans as to where we should try to settle, I should look at Topsham in Devon while I was in England. So, on a cold grey day with only seventy-two hours left before my return to Rhodesia, I found myself in Topsham with my sister Christine, hoping to find a house to rent. We booked in at the Globe Hotel and were struck by the beauty of the little riverside town on the Exe with its Dutch houses along the Strand.

However, we soon discovered that it was almost impossible to rent in Topsham. No agency existed for this purpose, nor were there any houses on the market. We wandered round the town getting more and more depressed and Chris felt that she really ought to be getting back to Dorset. I wanted to try once more, and as at that moment we were wandering up Monmouth Street, I decided to ring the bell of No. 36 on the off-chance that the occupants might know someone who was wanting to rent or sell. This seemed so unlikely that Chris thought I was crazy. However I did not feel that I had much to lose, and decided to follow my psychic instinct.

Plucking up courage, I rang the bell and the door was opened by the daughter of the house. To our amazement, she told us that her parents were intending to sell No. 36 shortly! Chris returned home and I stayed the night with the owners of the house, Mr and Mrs Shayler. They were very helpful and by the next day all was settled.

I borrowed the necessary £12,000 from my brother Brian, arranged with the Shayler's solicitors that they would manage the transaction, and agreed with the owners that they could stay in No. 36 until they found what they were looking for, as long as David, our youngest son who was now at Exeter University, could occupy their top spare room. This they agreed to and, thanks to my brother, everything went off smoothly and I was able to fly home the next day! The housing market in England started to leap up from that moment, and had I not bought 36 Monmouth Street when I did, we would have had no hope of raising the money to buy a house by the time we returned home at the end of 1971. This was the first of my 'psychic' property purchases in Topsham, all of which have benefited my family and me more than we could have imagined.

On my return to Rhodesia I found that things were becoming worse politically. The Centre Party newspaper which we published each month was in constant danger of being taken to court and as editor, I was responsible for the articles contained within it. As I have explained, it was against the law to print anything which, in the opinion of the government, would cause 'alarm and despondency'. It was therefore impossible for us to publish a political newspaper in opposition to the Rhodesia Front without breaking this law. Every edition carried warnings that the policies of the Government would lead to violence, if not to war, many of these articles being written by our African Members of Parliament and other thinking black Rhodesians, all of whom were beginning to give up hope.

Towards the end of 1971 we were sure that Rhodesia was no longer a place in which we could live. With the majority of the white population supporting a Government which seemed unaware that it was engineering the downfall of the country, there was no future for our children, who had been brought up to respect black Rhodesians. Also, my politics were endangering the family. 'Shotover', the house we had so caringly built on Mount Pleasant Drive, would have to be put up for sale, and the cottage on the Tsanga River in Inyanga would have to be left in the care of someone else. This turned out for the best when it was found that my sister-in-law's family could be there to look after it. The children and I had been very much against taking money for the cottage, for it was felt that such a blessed place should be shared with our friends and relations.

During 1971 we made our final plans to return to England. Restrictions were rigid about leaving the country and it was only possible to take £100 each if you were leaving permanently or £150 if you were going on holiday. We, of course, were 'going on holiday'!

It was laid down that only a minimum of household possessions (such as small objects which would be needed in a rented house) could be taken by those going abroad for further educational purposes. This applied to us, as Robert was taking another medical degree at the Royal Devon and Exeter Hospital. Nothing was allowed to be taken if you were leaving for good. However, I did not take any notice of such a restriction and went to a firm of exporters some months in advance, and arranged for them to come and pack up all that we wished to take and to send it to England. No-one seemed to take any notice! The rest of our possessions were sold at a garden sale in aid of the Centre Party.

I minded very much leaving my garden, which we had made from a totally wild bit of neglected land. We had planted many trees and worked to make it beautiful, but it had to go with the house and I prayed that those who bought it would care for it. We were lucky, for when I returned twenty-five years later it was very well cared for and the trees had grown to amazing heights.

The Shearly Cripps Home has progressed well, too, and when I was last in Rhodesia/Zimbabwe there were seventy-five children there. In the new State of Zimbabwe one of the worst problems which has now hit the Home is lack of work for the children who, because of their age, have to leave. The Home cannot keep children over eighteen years old and to send them away at that age means that they are bound to get into trouble. The only solution is to train them for some sort of work which can be supplied on the Mission, but lack of funds will always be the worst hurdle to overcome.

Our final departure from Salisbury was sad. We had many friends, in spite of my politics, and it felt as if we were rats leaving a sinking ship. I knew that we had to go because soon it would have become impossible for me to remain in a country which was steadily moving towards war with my black Rhodesian friends. Civil war is a terrible thing. If I had stayed I might have ended up in gaol, with all the family in Britain, and that would have served no purpose.

I had admired Guy Clutton-Brock (one of the founders of Rhodesia's Cold Comfort Farm Society) for his insistence, when he was notified that a Deportation Order was to be made against him, that he would never go voluntarily. I well recall seeing him the night he was deported from the country, walking across the tarmac of Salisbury Airport escorted by the police. The whole place was floodlit, police were everywhere, and thousands of Africans had come to bid Guy farewell, for he was deeply loved by the people all over the country. He left in November which, though warm in Africa, was going to be bitterly cold in England, but Guy would not take a coat or any luggage and was wearing a blue shirt and cotton trousers as he was escorted to the plane. He had done nothing except befriend the African farming community and try to help them to make a good living from the soil. Of course he openly opposed a Government which denied rights to the indigenous people, but he was a man of peace and only by an uncivilised Government could his actions have been seen as criminal.

Halfway across the runway Guy's escorting detective stopped holding him and immediately Guy stood still and refused to move. He was determined that he would not leave unless physically taken to the plane. He caused no violence, as he did not try to resist, but he was not going to go of his own free will. As he left their was a great burst of song from his friends on the top of the airport building singing 'Mwari Komborera Africa' (God bless Africa). Many people had come from the Inyanga District, two hundred miles away, with their leader, Chief Rekayi Tangwena, who was also under threat of arrest. Most of them were very old, very poor and dressed in old army greatcoats which enveloped them to their ankles. Their heads were wrapped in cloths to hide their faces from the police. Members of the Tangwena Tribe were in danger of arrest for refusing to get off the land of their ancestors, which was demanded by the Government for development.

We, the members of the Centre Party and others sympathisers, stood amongst these courageous people hoping to prevent their arrest. We did not believe that the police would make a move in such a public place, with such a large audience. When I spoke to the Chief himself and told him that I admired his stand to retain his homelands, he did not reply, but one of his escort explained, "He cannot speak English in the presence of the police." The man then looked over his shoulder at a group of well-dressed Africans standing close behind him. I said that I could see no police and the old man laughed and said "Many, many police with no uniforms." The group behind us looked embarrassed and turned their faces away.

The piping voices of the old men rang out across the airport as they sang 'We will overcome' accompanied by the many English-speaking people. Guy was escorted into the aircraft leaving his wife Molly to return to the farm. She had packed a small suitcase of clothes for him which was later put into the aircraft, for she knew he was going to need warm clothes when he got off the plane into the cold November weather of England. A cry of sadness and farewell rose from the crowd and the plane taxied away. Some of us wept. Wise people had arranged to spirit away the members of the Tangwena tribe in their cars directly the plane left. The men were escorted silently and no action was taken by the police, who had realised that any attempt to arrest the leaders would result in conflict, not only with the tribal members but with a large number of white Rhodesians who were prepared to stick their necks out. We left the airport in sorrow but with much admiration for the stand made by the Clutton-Brocks throughout their time in Africa, and the bravery shown by the Africans who came down from the mountains into 'enemy territory' in order to honour their friends.

When we were about to leave the country in 1971 I was still not aware that the South African banning order would prevent me from over-flying that country. However, as I had to land in Capetown in order to get to the ship, that was apparently sufficient reason to refuse permission. I wondered how the South African authorities thought I could damage the Republic from the air, but nevertheless the fact was that the Office of the Interior in Pretoria was not prepared to allow me to pollute their sacred airspace.

Robert and Clare left by train with all the luggage, while I remained in Salisbury wondering what on earth I was going to do. At the very last moment I was permitted to board an aircraft, on condition that I was escorted on and off the plane and was put into the hands of the purser when I reached the ship! Needless to say none of this occurred. No-one, to my knowledge, supervised my exit from Rhodesia and, on reaching Capetown, I found no escort. (This may have been because the spelling of the name by which they had listed me was incorrect, being Flynn instead of Fynn!) The purser of the ship had not received any instructions, but he assured me that he would have disregarded them in any case, it being a British ship. Had I really wanted to enter South Africa I could have done so at this point, for I passed through the barriers without trouble, none of the officials recognising me as a danger. After this our journey went smoothly.

When we arrived in England my next problem was to arrange with the British Government to grant citizenship to Robert and Clare, both of whom had been born in Rhodesia prior to UDI. This took some time but was eventually achieved. The same battle had been fought when, some years before, Richard and David had travelled to England. Richard was Rhodesian-born and had done his compulsory National Service in Rhodesia prior to the outbreak of the Rhodesian war. At that time entry into Britain was illegal for Rhodesian nationals and he was therefore immediately forbidden to land when his ship reached Southampton. He was looked on as an enemy alien and confined to the ship until his return to Rhodesia could be arranged. Luckily his elder brother, Peter, a British citizen by birth, could guarantee residence for him and take up the fight to allow him to remain in Britain, and we had good contacts. David, who arrived later, was coming over to England to go to University in Exeter. Determined not to fight his black school friends, he had left Rhodesia immediately after leaving school and before getting his call-up papers so as to avoid doing his National Service.

Richard and David were both granted nationalisation in the end, but only because I had close connections with the Foreign Office, having been in touch with them over the UDI travesty, and having been granted a special right to enter Britain during the negotiations. This right had been granted to me on an occasion when I came to London with Pat Bashford to see Sir Alec Douglas Home to discuss the deteriorating political situation between Britain and Rhodesia. I still have my British passport of that earlier time which contains a large crown stamped on one page and an order declaring that I am permitted to come and go from Rhodesia to Britain in spite of the general orders banning entrance from Rhodesia.

Gonville's Imprisonment

Soon after we arrived in England, Gonville was arrested in Johannesburg and sent to prison. He suffered badly in gaol as he was interrogated endlessly and allowed no visitors, not even his bishop. Nor was he allowed a Bible or any other reading matter. There had been a number of cases of sudden death of inmates in South African gaols at that time and he was fearful for his life. Later in England, after his release, he told me that he was interrogated by two men, one very tough and the other more reasonable. The 'nice guy' had long talks with him, trying to persuade him that the South African attitude to the African people was justified. This man said that they, the South Africans, rightly regarded the African people as animals. When the subject of mixed marriages came up, Gonville was told that it was forbidden in the Bible that men should cohabit with animals. Gonville was dumbfounded at this argument but he suddenly realised that to South Africans holding such profoundly wrong beliefs, the laws of their country must seem justified.

The outcry across the world at Gonville's arrest meant that the South African Government could not hold him for long without charge and he was eventually let out on the equivalent of £2000 bail, to await the result of his Appeal. The following letter came from Gonville to me in England, prior to his appeal in 1972.

My dear Diana,

Although you say that it is not necessary to write, I must just do so because your letters are a great comfort to me - and I'm so glad that you seem to be settling in so well in England - and it's winter too! I can't tell you how much I envy you!

Of course, if I go to prison, Laura will tell you about writing, [Laura was his wonderful and devoted secretary] *but I gather it is very tough - I think one is allowed about one letter a month or something like that. I know it's tougher in the first three months and then eases up a bit. However it may not come to that - I just don't know. The lawyers seem satisfied that they have gotten a very good and strong 'Heads of Argument' for the Appeal, but whether the judges will think so or not I don't know, nor does anyone know just how much 'politics' will enter into it all. It starts, as you know, on Feb 21st and is due to go on for two weeks - with the judgement probably being reserved for another three to four weeks, and I am not really enjoying the waiting around.*

*I am sure that you are wise to lie a bit fallow for six months
while you soak it all in and then get down to things and some
sort of plan. I can't help thinking that Paul Mashonaland has
boobed a bit over the 'Settlement' - I should think a lot of the
Africans will tend to walk out on him, which would be a pity -
but I'm not (in spite of what the judge says!) a politician.*

Yours ever and with much love,

Gonville.

When, eventually, he was taken to court to appeal against his
sentence, he was found not guilty and released. He flew back to England
that night, having been warned by a friend that he was likely to be
rearrested the following day on a further charge. On his arrival in
England I was able to meet him, and I found him in a nervous state, for he
had grown used to looking over his shoulder all the time. It took some
while for him to settle down, but he was soon installed as priest in
charge of a church near St Paul's Cathedral. I wondered if the
Archbishop of Canterbury had a sense of humour, putting a priest named
Gonville Aubie ffrench-Beytagh in charge of a parish church with the
equally unlikely name of 'St Vedast-alias-Foster'!

John Phillipps, 1790-1875, Harbour Master of Padstow, my great-great grandfather.

The marriage of my mother and father, Gwen and Freddy.

My eldest brother Peter, shortly before he died.

My grandmother, Christine (Kitty) Herbert Smith with her daughter Gwendolen, then aged sixteen - my mother.

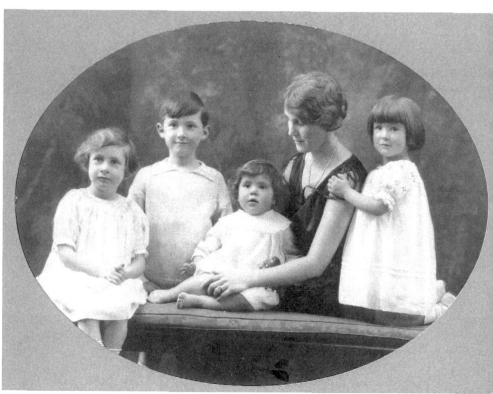

My mother with her first four children, Peter, Christine, Stella and myself (right).

Myself aged 18, when I first met Hugh.   F.O. Hugh Haswell in 1940, aged 21.

IN THIS CLOISTER
ARE RECORDED THE NAMES OF
TWENTY THOUSAND AIRMEN
WHO HAVE NO KNOWN GRAVE

GRAY J.A.
HARRIES G.
HASWELL H.
HAWORTH J.F.J.
HAWXBY N.

Hugh Haswell's name recorded with the 20,000 airmen with no known graves, Runnymede Memorial, Surrey.

'Shotover', Mt Pleasant Drive, Salisbury, Southern Rhodesia.

The Garden Cottage, 'Shotover'.

The Cottage at Inyanga,
Southern Rhodesia.

Gonville Aubrey ffrench-Beytagh,
when Dean of Salisbury Cathedral,
Southern Rhodesia.

Henri Leopold Dor, a close friend for thirteen years.

Clare and myself supervising the building of the Shearly Cripps Children's Home

The first intake of children to the Home.

The Fynn family in `Shotover'. *From left to right*: Robert, Peter, Sally, Richard, David, myself and Clare

Nine of my eldest grandchildren: Fynns, Jenningses (and a tenth, Jonathan, in cot).

My five children. *Clockwise from top left*: Sally, Richard, Peter, Clare, David.

Clare cutting Ted Fynn's hair, a few days before he died.

Four more grandchildren: *left*, Clare's children, Alexander, Sebastian and Marie-Claire Agertoft; *right*, Jonathan Fynn.

Myself at the Iron Bridge Art Centre run by Patrick and Bay Heriz-Smith.

Clay head of Clare aged 17, waiting to be cast in bronze. By D.F.

'Scaffold': oil on board. By D.F.

James Smeall in his
garden at Follett
Orchard, Topsham.

Myself in old age, reading someone else's book.

Chapter 29

Family Life in Devon

Our return to England at the end of 1971 was not as traumatic as it might have been because of course we had a house to go to: 36 Monmouth Street in Topsham. It was a dear little house and we fitted in easily, partly because we had very little furniture! Our possessions took many weeks to arrive from Africa and in the meantime we made do with borrowed beds, the few things which had travelled with us, and the packing cases they came in.

Clare settled in at the junior school as a day pupil, although she found that the work was below the level she had reached in Rhodesia, but she enjoyed her time there and made many friends. The winter was quite mild that year which was lucky as the transition from Africa to Britain could have been difficult. Robert took temporary locum work in Exeter but soon managed to join the staff of the Royal Devon and Exeter Hospital. This meant that he had to do night as well as day duties, but the job brought in a steady income which was very necessary. The British Government had closed all Rhodesian bank accounts in Britain because of UDI, but in anticipation of this I had arranged with my mother and father some years before that they should cease to pay my small allowance into my account, and place it instead in my mother's bank. This was a wise move as the amount of money which my mother held for me by the time we arrived amounted to about £3000.

I was hopeful that our new life in a new place would result in a happier family situation. The constant threats to our marriage in the past had been hard to take and only the fact of five children, and the financial impossibility of leaving Africa, had kept me there. Gonville ffrench-Beytagh's belief that marriage was sacred and that our vows were for life, in spite of how often they might be broken by either partner, had encouraged me to stay and do my best to bring up the children in a secure family home. I have never ceased to be thankful for his advice, because Clare would not have been born had I left.

Soon after our arrival in Devon, David, who had been living at 36 Monmouth Street for his final year at Exeter University, left for the United States to marry a girl called Carol Witwer. He had met her at the University on an exchange programme. Peter was married to Gill, who had come with me to so many Centre Party meetings in Rhodesia, while Sally had married a priest called David Jennings. Interestingly, Richard was to meet his future wife at his brother's wedding in America.

At this time I opened a toy shop in Topsham called 'The Hobbit Hole'. Never having had any experience of running a business, I was soon having to cope with the transition to decimal currency and with VAT! The shop was fun, but also remarkably successful. It was not an ordinary toy shop, for most of the toys came from unusual sources and were reminiscent of the Victorian era. I made use of many local talents and was helped by a number of people who produced handmade wooden toys.

One was Dr. Alan Staniland, who had retired from Exeter University. He made charming miniature replicas of furniture which he had seen in the various houses and museums he visited. Later he made beautiful doll's houses, one of which I could not bring myself to sell. It is a copy of a Regency house in St Leonard's Road in Exeter and is entirely equipped by him with charming furniture in keeping with its architecture: it now belongs to Clare.

Eric Horne was another blessing to me, as he agreed to try his hand at making 'Dutch dolls', wooden articulated dolls originally known as 'deutsch dolls' and made in the Black Forest area of Germany. He became so successful that he now has his own toy-making business based on these miniature wooden dolls, which are beautifully made and sell in America as fast as he can make them. Amongst my collection I have one he gave me which measures 7 mm, is fully articulated and has to live in a tiny hardwood egg for safety. It is one of my most precious possessions. Later Eric turned to making a few Pedlar Dolls which carried quantities of minute toys on their trays and which, by now, must be of great value. He also visited France to meet other toymakers, one of whom wrote books on antique toys and wanted him to make copies of humming tops and other toys.

I had sailed a great deal in my youth and had owned a 22-ft Norfolk Racing Gun Punt on which I had learnt much about dinghy sailing, so during the next few years we sailed on the Exe Estuary. We owned a variety of different boats. Robert had never sailed much but I had imported a Flying Dutchman into Rhodesia which we sailed on a local dam and the boys had become excellent dinghy sailors. However river sailing was very different from racing on the Norfolk Broads or the Mazoe Dam in Central Africa, and we had to learn the ways of the estuary tides. The sea lay beyond the Exmouth sandbanks and it took careful calculation if one was to go down and come back with the tide.

Despite the fact that living in Topsham was wonderful and we were both thankful that we had returned to England, the years between 1972 and 1978 became fraught with repeated events which convinced me that, from the point of view of our marriage, living in England was going to be no less distressing than the life we had left. Robert had taken up a job in the Casualty Department at the Royal Devon and Exeter Hospital and this meant that his nights were frequently spent in residence. I realised that he had to take the job as we were desperately short of money, but I also knew that he was spending too much time away from home and our marriage was under constant threat.

Chapter 30

The Death of My Parents

When my father retired, my parents had gone to live in Jersey. Now my father was seriously ill and going downhill fast. He had what would now be diagnosed as Alzheimer's disease, but was then known as senility. He had been a very energetic man, full of ideas and a great one for making friends, but now my mother kept him closely guarded at home and neither of them went out very much, which was not good for her. His mother had suffered in the same way in her old age but, having plenty of help in the house and devoted servants who stayed with her until the end, she had never had to go into a home.

My father's behaviour became more and more bizarre and it was hard for my mother to cover it up. Because Jersey had been occupied by the Nazis during the war, his illness made him suspicious of anyone in uniform. He became convinced that the postman was a Nazi spy, and stood at his bedroom window determined to shoot him. If my mother had not hidden the ammunition for his old service revolver there might have been a serious accident. She showed immense courage throughout his illness. When the time came that the illness prevented him from recognising her, it caused her enormous pain and when he died she never really recovered from losing him, for they had been the most devoted couple. She laughed and cried at the same time when she told me some of the difficult situations she had had to deal with. One night when she was reading in bed he had come in and ordered her out of the room saying, "Gwen will be horrified if she comes back and finds a strange woman in our bed." Nothing my mother could say would change his mind and he pushed her outside into the garden in her nightdress and closed the front door. She stood there in the dark not knowing what to do, but eventually she rang the front-door bell. When my father came down and opened the door he was overjoyed to see her, and told her that some awful woman had been in her bed and he had only just been able to get rid of her. He seemed to be unaware that she was still in her nightdress. I suppose it was a great relief to her that he was so thankful to have her back, but she had to carry a heavy burden of such incidents until one night he died peacefully in his sleep.

My mother did not live many years without him. Like her two sisters, she died unexpectedly in her sleep having had no illness or warning. My father and mother are both buried in the little churchyard of St. Brelades Church in Jersey in the same grave as his mother and father. The grave was bought by my grandfather when he and his wife retired to Jersey after the Great War. In those days buying a burial plot was one of the ways of declaring your domicile in the Channel Islands. When my grandparents came to live in Jersey, they discussed the pros and cons of the various grave sites suggested by the vicar, and my grandfather agreed to buy one. My grandmother, however, was not satisfied with his choice. She took him aside and said, "Not that one, Fred dear. There is a tree close by and I think we might find it rather damp."

Chapter 31

Revolution in Nicaragua

Early in 1970 my son Peter, his wife Gill and their two children, Tamsen and Nicholas, had gone to live in Nicaragua. The children were quite small but Peter's work took him abroad and both he and Gill were keen to help the Third World. Not long after their arrival the situation in the country went from bad to worse and a revolution erupted, caused by the dictator Somoza whose evil rule had bankrupted Nicaragua and caused starvation to the people. Peter and Gill were in a difficult position but they were unable to leave until all their debts had been paid. As their business had been forcibly closed by the state of violence in Managua, it was not easy to settle their debts, and the law in Nicaragua sent debtors straight to prison without option.

In 1978 I flew from Heathrow to Madrid and thence to Nicaragua. It was a harrowing journey for me, as I was aware that things would probably go badly wrong at home while I was away. However, I reached Peter and Gill successfully and was able to help financially in a small way. Just before my arrival Peter had had an altercation with the Nicaraguan policeman who owned their rented property. There were no locks on the doors and the policeman was running a brothel in the servants' quarters alongside the house. The situation was intolerable and Peter had refused to pay the rent until things improved. The result was that he had been threatened by the owner and one day, as they were driving through the city, his car had been shot at by a policeman on a motorbike. A bullet had gone under the seat on which Gill was sitting.

Peter had put his foot down, turned the car the wrong way up a one-way street, quickly driven into a garage belonging to a friend and closed the doors. When I arrived a few weeks later they were both still shaken by the incident, which had only been resolved by the arrival of an

American lawyer who offered to help them. He had come to the country in an official government capacity and was therefore in a strong position. Peter was called to the Central Police Station and went on the assurance of the lawyer that he would be safe. The case was investigated and the policeman in question disappeared!

I made the most of my few weeks in Nicaragua by seeing some of the country, camping up in the mountains with the family in a hut owned by friends, and climbing a volcano. The camp was at a place called Buaco and the hut was on the edge of a forest inhabited by colonies of howler monkeys, where there were also vampire bats. Nicholas, my small grandson, very kindly warned me about the bats and told me to keep my toes under the blankets, as I was sleeping on the verandah.

Early one morning as I walked in the forest I watched a sloth, with a young one clinging below it, meandering slowly along under the branch of a forest tree. It was not easy to see because its coat was covered in green, hanging moss which grew upon it owing to the warm dampness in the air. I was also screamed at by howler monkeys during my early walks. The monkeys were interesting, quite large and very noisy, but they were also rather frightening. They suddenly appeared overhead in the forest in large numbers, screaming at rival colonies as they tried to establish their right of possession to certain trees. I stood below their battleground and watched amazed as they taunted each other and occasionally turned their attention to me. When I returned to breakfast Nicholas, who was about seven years old, asked me if they had peed on me. Apparently this was what they usually did if you invaded their territory!

Peter and I drove up the nearest volcano as far as the road would allow and then climbed to the top and looked into the crater. I could not stand and look down, for fear of falling into the cauldron of molten rock which was surging in red, flaming waves hundreds of feet below, so we crawled forward to the edge and watched spellbound for some time. Brilliant green parrots circled the inside of the crater and came to rest in noisy groups on the rock walls.

The Nicaraguan people were charming and the children incredibly beautiful but the poverty was dreadful and the country was verging on revolution. I flew home to England very concerned for the future of the country and for my son and his family. They eventually managed to get out at a moment's notice and, negotiating barricades on the road to the airport, caught a plane which landed in New Orleans. Luckily, my brother Ian was head of the Raleigh Bicycle Company which had offices in that city. I had been in touch with him, and through his office was able to help Peter and Gill with some finance to buy an old van which would get them up to Ohio. Once there, they found their way to the town of Willoughby where they were welcomed by my son David's parents-in-law, the Witwers. In fact, the yellow van in which they made that trip north remained their only means of transport for many years. In the winter their feet froze onto the floor until they bought some cheap, fluffy, yellow material and lined the whole van with this strange, woolly carpet.

Chapter 32

An Impossible Situation

On my return from Nicaragua I realised that the situation at home had deteriorated and it was apparent that my marriage was coming to an end, but I delayed any action until Clare went to boarding school at the age of sixteen.

Robert was spending more and more time away from home. 'Meetings' in Torquay and London and other unidentified places took up much of his time. I was not told where these 'meetings' were nor the purpose of them, but it was not hard to discover that they were unofficial. It may seem strange that I did not leave then and there, as I found this rejection deeply hurtful, but the outlook was bleak financially and there was Clare to consider.

I was in such a state of depression during this period of my life, that one night, when Robert was out until after three o'clock in the morning, and I was alone in the house with Clare asleep upstairs in the attic bedroom, I took an overdose. I had been sitting awaiting his return for hours and was overwhelmed by a growing sense of distress; it seemed as if the walls of the room where moving inwards and darkness was overtaking me. I began to collect as many pills as I could lay my hands on, not even knowing what they were or how many I was taking. I only knew that I could endure this unhappiness no longer and had to find a way out. I can only imagine, in retrospect, that I had broken down at last after all the years of struggling to keep my family together. That Clare was in the house and would be the first one to find me did not enter my head. I realise now that I was 'of unsound mind'.

Having swallowed a quantity of the pills, I went round the house closing and locking all the doors and windows, but suddenly I lost my balance and fell on the floor in the hall. It was there that Robert must have discovered me in the early hours of the morning when he finally got in by climbing through the small window in the back lavatory. I knew nothing about this until I heard Robert shouting at me to wake up eighteen hours later. He had taken Clare to school that morning and gone to work leaving me in the house alone. I had evidently not taken a sufficient number of pills to kill myself, but far too many to have been left alone with the remaining pills still beside my bed. When I surfaced sufficiently to realise what I had done, I begged Robert to stay with me that evening, but he left again to go to another 'appointment'.

This experience enabled me to relate to the state of mind into which people have to sink in order to try to commit suicide. It has given me an understanding of many incomprehensible actions taken by people in distress, and a knowledge of the true meaning of the phrase 'of unsound mind'. Suicide is certainly not the sin which it has been described as by the church. I realise that my actions at that time were really a call for help to some unknown source, and that desperation can lead one into a dark hole out of which it seems impossible to climb.

Some months later I had a dream, which I am including here as I believe that it demonstrates the powerful effect of precognitive dreaming. I had gone to bed prepared to get up at five-thirty as I was going to London on the early train. On waking, I told Robert that I would not go after all because I had had a vivid and frightening dream, which had been so real that I felt as though it was really going to happen. He asked me what it was about and I told him,

"In the dream I found myself walking down the stairs which led to the platform of a railway station. Below me I saw your mistress standing facing me with two suitcases beside her; I was about to board the same train as she was. I panicked and started to run back the way I had come. Someone behind me, I do not know who, put their hands firmly on my shoulders and turned me round telling me that I had to speak to her, and I woke up."

Robert dismissed the whole thing as rubbish and said that the woman in question was not off work that day and could not be on the train. I was very shaken, but eventually, after some deliberation, I decided to go ahead with my original plans. I left the house telling myself not to be hysterical.

When I reached the station I was still apprehensive, for I was afraid to meet the woman. She had been violent to me on one occasion in the past and she was a very real threat to my family. However, there was no sign of her on the platform and I tried to dismiss the dream as being caused by my disturbed state of mind at that time. I boarded the train and walked to the front where I found a seat in an empty carriage, and leaving my newspaper there, I went to the dining car for breakfast.

On my return the carriage seemed empty, but when I reached my seat I saw that the one opposite mine was occupied. *The woman in my dream faced me across the table between our seats.*

Apart from the two of us the carriage was empty. She could not have known that I was on the train or that I was due to return to that particular seat, for I had left only a newspaper to mark my place and had no luggage by which she could have identified me. She was as surprised as I was and for a moment we just sat and looked at each other. She was embarrassed, but told me that she had caught the train at the last moment and had walked to the front in order to be near the barrier at Paddington. I had gone to get breakfast before the train left the station and she had not had to pass through the dining car so she could not have seen me there.

My first reaction was to move to another part of the train but I recalled the voice in my dream which had told me to speak to her, so I picked up my paper and sat down. I remained there as far as Taunton, during which time it was she who spoke, rather than I. I was forced to listen to a detailed description of her times with my husband, which I found intolerable, and was about to move to another seat when the train stopped and the carriage was filled with a horde of school children for which it had apparently been reserved.

The rest of the journey took a further two hours during which time she slowly but surely destroyed any faith that I might have had left in my marriage. She described how she and Robert had planned secret meetings, how they had slept together in the hospital on night duty, had holidayed together when he was meant to be at conferences, and how she had slept in my bed when I was away helping to nurse my father. She was determined that she would leave no stone unturned to cause the breakup of my marriage, and I left the train feeling destroyed.

In London I changed my plans and decided to take the Underground to St. Paul's instead of going to the Royal Academy as planned. I had only one hope, and that was that I would be able to find Gonville ffrench-Beytagh at home in his vicarage. I left Paddington Station and climbed the stairs to the City Line.

I had already realised that the woman had not appeared quite as she had done in the beginning of my dream, when she was standing on a station platform with her luggage. However, as I walked out onto the platform of the Underground which would take me to St. Paul's, I looked up and saw her standing on the opposite platform across the railway lines. She had two suitcases beside her and appeared just as she had in the dream.

In the dream the events had not been shown in the order in which they actually occurred, but there is no normal time in dreaming. The fact of seeing her on the opposite platform was clearly the experience which led me into the dream. A dream is described as 'precognitive' when it gives us an insight into an event which will occur in *what we in this world understand to be* the future. Another precognitive dream of great consequence is recorded earlier in this book at the time of the death of my fiancé, Hugh, in 1940.

The dream of the woman on the platform was one of the most dramatic and clear-cut dreams I have ever had. It seemed to be acted out as if on a stage set. There was no room for doubt, no possibility that I had invented it after the event, for I had told Robert exactly what I had dreamt two hours before it began to unfold in reality. The dream showed me that I could no longer survive alone with him when Clare went off to boarding school, and confirmed that all my efforts to save my marriage had been in vain. I believe this was the purpose of the dream: to make me see that I was wasting my time trying to restore life to a dead situation.

I did not want to take sudden drastic action. My mother, who was not recovering well from the death of my father, would have been devastated to know of the breakup of my marriage. In the end I waited until Clare was older and shortly to go to boarding school before telling her what plans I had made for the future. She was a wise child and realised that things were very difficult between Robert and myself, and she accepted what I was trying to say in a very adult way.

Chapter 33

A Sudden Death

An uncomfortable period ensued with Robert living in a flat while I tried to keep the house going as a home for Clare, who was enjoying boarding school. However, Robert and I were living too close for comfort, and bits and pieces kept disappearing from my house to stock his flat until in the end I had to change the locks. All the dining-room furniture had gone over to him together with the contents of his study and the spare bedroom, and as his was only a two-roomed flat it was pretty crowded. However, Clare and I managed very well without a dining room, spare room or study.

It was sometime during this period that Ted, Robert's elder brother, came to Britain from Portugal. He was a very sick man. When he had separated from his first wife, the mother of his four children, he had left Rhodesia, and he was now living with a second wife whom I hardly knew. They had nowhere to go and were penniless. At this time Robert was living in a house belonging to his mistress, and Ted and his wife stayed with them.

A few months later, unexpectedly, and in spite of Ted's terminal illness, Robert suddenly decided to return to Rhodesia to live with someone else and to join a medical practice there. This caused chaos. The woman who owned the house was infuriated and indulged in fierce rows, and when Robert finally left for Africa, Ted and his wife were turned out with nowhere to go. Ted phoned me asking if I could suggest anywhere they might live. Until this point I had not realised that they were homeless, but now I was delighted to take them in. I would have had them before but, according to Ted, Robert had said that I would not want them. I had always been devoted to Ted, although when he had left his wife and family all those years before it had made me very angry and I had told him so.

My home by that time was No. 48 The Strand in Topsham, a lovely little Regency house on the edge of the river Exe. I had bought it after Robert left me. Ted arrived looking desperately ill but brightened up a lot as he sat in the garden and watched the boats coming and going on the river. He had been a great sailor and had always had dreams of making long sea journeys, which sadly never came off. The moment I saw him I realised that he was terminally ill and wondered how Robert could have left with Ted in such a state.

During the three weeks which led up to his death Ted and I were able to have many important talks, for we had been very fond of each other in the past. Since the rift between us when he left his family, we had not had a chance to meet, so now we made good use of the little time left. Ted also had a chance to meet a close friend of mine, Henri Leopold Dor, who frequently came down to Topsham from London. Ted and Henri Leopold had much to say to each other and, in spite of Ted's serious condition, they managed to find many points of contact in the beliefs and knowledge which they had both accumulated in the course of their lives. Their last meeting was the day before Ted's death.

Ted's leaving of this life was dramatic and rather in keeping with the way he had lived. He was a remarkable man and had great courage which helped him through the drama of his going. At about three in the morning I was called by his wife to say that Ted was haemorrhaging. His cancer, which was in the bronchial tubes, had perforated the heart wall and there was no possible way that the bleeding could be stopped. As I watched by him it quickly developed into a torrent of blood and he sat on the side of the bed with his large hands on his knees and gave himself to the moment. He never complained.

I sat on the bed beside him with my arms round him holding him up, hoping that he would lose consciousness more quickly when the remaining blood in his body could no longer reach his brain. I had told his wife that he was going fast and she came over and sat on the other side of him. I had sent for my doctor but he was away, and the doctor who came had no knowledge of the case. He merely sent for an ambulance and left soon afterwards, giving Ted's wife some pills to help her to sleep through the rest of the night. (Later I gathered that, unknown to anyone, this doctor was beginning to suffer from a serious brain illness himself and was not really able to cope with such a traumatic situation. He had, in the past, been one of the most caring and capable doctors in the town).

As Ted became weaker I spoke softly to him as I held him in my arms, so that he would know that he was not alone. His blood flowed over us both and within a short time he had gone. Never before had I had the experience of knowing just when the spirit leaves the body. It was unmistakable: one moment I held Ted close to me and the next he was no longer there. His body had become an empty shell, yet he was still upright and had not moved his hands from his knees as he sat on the edge of the bed beside me. I felt that he had given me a great gift, in that I should have been present at such an overwhelming event. I laid him back on the bed and suggested to his wife that she should rest in my room while I tried to clear up and waited for the ambulance to arrive.

Some time later the ambulance came, but the men who came with it were young and perhaps not very experienced. They took one look at the chaos in the room and the blood-soaked towels lying on the floor and told me to send for the police. I eventually convinced them that Ted had died of natural causes and they helped me to get him back onto the bed and straighten his limbs. They could not take him away because they were only allowed to transport living patients. I covered Ted with a sheet and for the rest of the night I sat on the stairs in a state of shock, my immediate concern being that I must somehow arrange for him to be taken away before Clare, who was asleep in the attic room, came down for breakfast. Ted's wife was still asleep in my bed, having taken the pills left by the doctor.

I must have dozed off on the stairs for a while because I suddenly came to, thinking that maybe I had made a mistake and Ted was not dead. This was, of course, quite impossible, but I went back into the room and turned back the sheet which covered him. His eyes, which had been closed when I left him, had opened and he was looking straight at me. I could barely control the primitive fear that overcame me and, covering his face, I fled from the room. Later, as the morning light began to touch the river beyond the garden, I was ashamed of my reaction. Had he been alive I would have been compassionate. Why, then, was I so shocked by his corpse?

Early in the morning I went to the phone and called the town undertaker, Mr Turl, who sent people to take Ted's body to the mortuary. Later Mr Turl came round again and helped me to clear up. He was a great strength to me, taking away everything which could be removed and assuming responsibility for all the technicalities of dealing with Ted's death.

I had to find the courage to ring up Ted's family in Rhodesia and tell them he had died. This was not easy, as they were all devoted to him and had not been prepared by Robert for his death. His daughter, Vanessa, answered the phone, and guessed at once what I had rung up to say. She became hysterical and I could do nothing to help her, but Viv, his first wife, was able to hear most of the details of his dying. It was not easy: all I could say to them was that his going was swift and that he had been incredibly brave. He had not been in pain and the shock of dying in this way was less for him than for those around him. However frightening it had seemed to those with him, he had quietly faded from his life and shown no struggle to breathe. He was an exceptional man.

Two of Ted's children, Vanessa and Mike, arrived from Rhodesia for the funeral, and some days after the cremation we went down to where the river Otter joins the sea and sent Ted on his way as he would have wished. It was a warm but wild and windy night and Vanessa sat on the shingle beach holding the small plastic box of ashes on her lap. We ate a picnic supper while the waves roared against the cliffs and flooded up the mouth of the river. We drank wine and laughed at our stories about Ted, and remembered what a loveable person he had been. Finally Mike, his younger son, stood above the water's edge, and while we all said a short prayer, cast the ashes into the air. They were picked up by the wind and shone in the moonlight, spreading like a silver cloud, before they fell onto the surface of the river and were washed out to sea by the tide.

Two days after Ted's death I woke early in the morning and in the half light I saw Ted beside my bed. He moved towards the back wall of the room but stopped when I spoke to him. I said in distress, "Oh, Ted, I have sent away your body. It is no longer in there," but he smiled and, by a gesture, indicated that he had no need of it. He passed on through the wall and into the room where he had died and where his wife was sleeping. I did not tell her that I had seen him but when, later, I asked her if she had felt that Ted was close, she said she had not.

On this occasion, and in earlier encounters I have had when knowledge was passed into my mind without speech, I seemed to understand and to recall the meaning very clearly. However it has always been difficult to translate the knowledge into words. The exception to this was the time in Rhodesia, all those years before, when a child was saved. On that occasion the message was actually spoken through me, using my own mouth to enunciate the words. This was because the message was urgent and had to be understood by a third person. When the communication comes through the mind, it is as if one has been in a foreign country where it is briefly possible to understand the language, but on returning home, translating the memory of the message into words becomes almost impossible without losing the wisdom it contained.

Chapter 34

A Near Death Experience?

During the winter of 1981, I had booked to go over to Kent to attend a meeting of Centre Space, a group to which I belonged. We were to be addressed by a healer who had a very good reputation and I really wanted to go. However, I was recovering from flu and the thought of driving all that way now that the weather had turned bitterly cold filled me with dread. I rang up to cancel, but in the end was persuaded to come in spite of the weather. The journey from Devon was awful and I arrived in Kent tired and cold.

The healer gave us instruction in her art - or perhaps I should say, gift - with several talks and demonstrations during the weekend. I had been interested in spiritual healing for a long time but had not practised it. Towards the end of the time she offered to help any of us who would like to be given healing and I was encouraged by friends to go forward.

I had watched her place her hands above the bodies of one or two other people as they lay on her demonstration table, but it was not possible to know whether her healing had had any effect. When it was my turn I lay face down on her portable table. The healer did not know me and had no knowledge of any of the problems I had had over the years. Her hands did not touch me, but when they were above the lumbar region of my spine, she said that I had had a lot of trouble there, but that it was not giving me any pain at the present time. This was true, and made me hopeful of her ability.

Reaching the upper spine between my shoulder blades she touched me with one finger on the exact spot where I had been having a great deal of pain, but which was not causing trouble at that moment. She told me that I had had pain from two pinched nerves, but that they were now released and would not give me any more trouble. Later on this turned out to be true. She then asked me to turn over onto my back and I saw her hands lift over me, but at that moment something strange happened.

I found that I had left my body and was floating in what appeared to be water but did not feel like water. In fact I seemed to have no bodily feeling at all. This was probably because the form I was in was not a normal body. As I floated on a slow moving current I looked down the length of where I expected my body to be, but it was not visible, only indicated by a gentle movement on the surface. I wondered if I had a face, but without a mirror I had no means of telling. The river, for that was what it seemed to be, was flowing slowly through what appeared to be a cave, the rounded roof of which was five or six feet above me, and there was a faint glow from the water reflected on the surface of the curved, stone roof.

I was moving towards a distant light, although I am not sure how I knew this as I was not facing the way the river was taking me. I was aware of a great sense of peace and wholeness: I had no worries and no memory of grief, only a great desire to travel the way I was going. Until the moment of entering this new dimension I had been obsessed with illness, worries and fears for the future and deep grief for the past, but they had all vanished as though they had never been. I felt totally well and perfectly safe. This does not mean that I had no memories at all: I was aware that I would have to go on without Clare, but even this did not disturb me. I also knew who I was, although I would not like to define such knowledge.

I do not know how long I remained in this state, for there was no sense of time. Then, from the far distance, I heard a voice calling, "Come back! You must come back. You have gone too far."

It was a human voice and it sounded urgent. I knew that it was calling me back to the life I had so willingly left. I did not want to obey, but felt compelled to return.

The way back was strange. I did not travel by the way I had come but felt myself falling suddenly from a height towards the room where my body lay. I could see it below me, but could not imagine how I was going to regain possession of it. The process by which I achieved re-entry is not easy to recall. I faintly remember focusing on the head as it lay on the table and using my mind to aid my return; it is also probable that the power of the Healer helped my re-entry.

When I found myself back on the table I became aware that I was unable to move. It was as if I had been placed in a straightjacket. This was frightening, but I was able to speak to the healer who told me to keep calm until I felt that things were back to normal. After a while I was able to move again and, with help, was able to get up off the table. The healer asked me whether I knew that I too was a healer, and added, "You should use this gift."

I felt vague and unable to understand what had happened, and returned to my place. The girl sitting beside me said she agreed with the healer, but I was too bemused to take in anything until after the meeting, when I asked her to repeat to me what the healer had said. Sadly, I did not follow this up by speaking to the healer myself about my experience, nor do I recall discussing it with any of the other people at the meeting, probably because I could find no words to explain what had occurred.

This was in 1981, and at the time I was not aware that other people had undergone similar experiences. I had not read any books on the subject and the expression 'Near Death Experience' (or *NDE*) was not known to me. There was no doubt in my mind that I had left my body and had travelled towards somewhere, something, or someone for which, or for whom, I longed. I knew that in the process I had been healed and released from the tensions and mental trauma from which I had been suffering. I remembered clearly being without a body and beyond time, and also being called back from the journey I was on, but that was all. It seemed that the sound of the voice calling to me had come from a different place, but in the strange circumstances in which I found myself, despite being unwilling to obey, I had no option but to return.

Since that time, over the years, I have come across many examples of similar events. The thing which interests me about my experience is that it did not happen, as it usually does, when the subject is seriously ill, under drugs, or involved in an accident. I was not near death, and yet ever since that moment I have lost all fear of death and dying and, in fact, would welcome it as age creeps up on me. I have been been with those who are dying and I have sometimes been present at the moment of death, but never have I seen anyone die in fear. In the twenty years since this NDE, perhaps more correctly described in my case as an EHE (Exceptional Human Experience), I have had opportunities to reassure many people about the reality of life after death and I believe that it was for this purpose that I was given this experience. In retrospect I can see it as a foretaste of the remarkable events which were to happen later in my life.

Chapter 35

Life After Divorce

In 1979 Robert had gone to live with someone else in Zimbabwe. Three years later he started divorce proceedings against me on the grounds of incompatibility. I had held out against divorce for some time because I could not see the point of it, when we had been married for nearly forty years and had five children and thirteen grandchildren. A legal separation seemed a more civilised decision and did not require the breaking of our vows, and in any case I could not see how *his* numerous infidelities could justify his divorcing *me* as incompatible. However, he was in Zimbabwe and had no intention of coming home. He had been living with someone he had known for a long time, having returned to her in 1979, and they wanted to get married.

Reluctantly I signed the papers and regained sole possession of my house, which I had bought with money borrowed from my brother when we first came to England, but which, at that time, I had put into both our names. After nearly forty years of marriage, having his children, running his home and helping him with his practice over many years, ownership of my house was all I was going to get and I had to be content with it. Clare was sixteen and happy at boarding school and it was not going to make any difference to her in the long run. The other children, all of whom were married and settled in their own homes, were sad but accepted it as inevitable.

I turned my mind to painting and sculpture and joined the Iron Bridge Art Centre in Exeter. Here I made many friends, particularly Bay and Patrick Heriz-Smith, whose teaching has brought back to life so many people in need of positive thinking. They have now retired, but I still recall the hilarious hours I spent with Bay and the other students as we struggled to build pots and sculptures. My most successful effort was a clay head of Clare which I decided to have cast in bronze, and with which I drove to London to find a casting foundry under the railway bridges in Clapham. It was a tense journey, because she would have fallen on her face if I had had to stop in a hurry and months of work would have been destroyed, but she had to be cast in the clay while damp in order to prevent shrinkage. She now stands in bronze in Clare's house.

Clay Pots

Cool silken smooth
with hands clay shaping
lifting above the wheel, soft,
grey and wet with dew
to aid its making.

Scent of deep earth
all nature in the baking.
I think of infant elephants in
mud holes sloshing, grey
clay-cooled bodies
under tropic sun.

So, my small object
rising from the surface,
pot-bellied, soft, unsteady
needing gentle care and
nurturing, as they.

During the winter of 1980, after Robert left and Ted died, I was depressed. Due largely to the friendship of Henri Leopold, however, who frequently came over to talk with me, I began to come out of the acute unhappiness which had followed the events of the previous year. I went to work for 'Crisis at Christmas' in the East End of London over the Christmas period, which was a good way to spend that particular season.

At 'Crisis at Christmas' I witnessed the problems which many down-and-outs were experiencing throughout their lives. One very elderly lady who arrived at the Centre was dressed in an Edwardian costume, the colour of which was unidentifiable as it can never have visited the cleaners. She also wore a silver-coloured toque which had suffered the same fate. Her possessions filled two plastic bags, which she stowed safely under her chair. She sat bolt upright all night long on a hard wooden chair, and when I suggested to her that I could find her a mattress to lie on she said in a shocked, Cockney voice, "Wha'? With all these men in the room? They'd jump you as soon as look at you! I wouldn't feel safe."

I assured her that we would look after her if she fell asleep, but she refused the offer. Amongst the crowd in the hall there were various young Irish boys, one of whom talked to me off and on through most of the night. He was homesick but had spent his last penny coming to London. I asked him what he did with the weekly cash he got from the Government and he said, "Bless you, and am I not drinking it?"

For the three days of Christmas I ferried huge quantities of boiled potatoes and other vegetables from distant kitchens to the central kitchen beside the main hall. Turkey stew slopped over into the boot of my car and the smell became awful. At the end of the three days I rushed to a friend's house and had a long hot bath and a change of clothes before driving back to Devon, but my car never quite recovered.

Chapter 36

Henri Leopold Dor

During this period I had become great friends with a neighbour called Miss Dorothy Holman, who lived in an old house across the road from where I lived on the Strand in Topsham. She was ninety years old, rather lame, but incredibly quick mentally. When I first knew her she was living with her sister, Madame Dor, but shortly after we met her sister died and Dorothy had to manage on her own. She was glad to have my company whenever I had the time, but seemed equally content to be alone.

Henri Leopold Dor, who had been so kind to me and to Ted, was Dorothy's nephew. At the time we met he lived in London, but came down frequently to see her and it was on one of these occasions that we were introduced.

Henri Leopold (or HL, as he was known to many people) was a striking man. His father was French and had been a well-known barrister in his own country. HL had also read law at Cambridge but was unable to practise as a lawyer owing to damaged hearing, caused by illness as a child and torture when in the hands of the Gestapo during the Second World War. He revealed little about his time in the French Resistance, with whom he had worked undercover, moving between France and Italy in secret until finally captured by the Italians. He spoke to me only once about how he had been caught in Milan and delivered to the Germans when Italy pulled out of the war. The records of the details of his capture were not handed over with him, which was just as well, for had they been, or had the Gestapo managed to break him when they tried to obtain information from him under torture, he would have been shot, for he had been caught in possession of a radio.

After his transfer from the Italians into the hands of the Gestapo he was imprisoned in a chateau in Nice and subjected to torture in the basement of the house. When he first arrived he was locked in a small cell with nothing but a bed, and a lavatory basin in the corner of the room. Soon he became aware of tapping coming from the corner by the lavatory. He was able to pick up a faint message telling him to ladle the water out of the lavatory pan in order to hear what his contact was saying. He did this, and discovered that the man in the next cell was a friend who had been with him at Cambridge University! This made his imprisonment much easier to bear as, through this contact, he was able to find out details about the other prisoners. HL had a gift for story-telling and wrote a series of fairy-stories on tiny bits of lavatory paper which were distributed to his cell-mates by a sympathetic French warder. Each edition was eagerly awaited by the other prisoners and as time went by he became known as 'l'Enchanteur'.

One of the forms of torture used by the Gestapo was to string a net across the stairwell of the house and spreadeagle prisoners upon it, tied by their wrists and ankles. HL was left like this for many hours, but far worse was the frequent experience, in the basement lavatories beneath the house, of being beaten until he lost consciousness. He told me that he managed to leave his body on occasions and watch his torturers from the ceiling. In this way he was able to avoid some of the pain. It was during one of these beatings that his eardrum was damaged, which was the reason for some of the deafness he suffered for the rest of his life.

How long he was confined in this prison he never told me, but he did reveal that during one bout of torture he lost consciousness and was sent to hospital in a coma. It was intended that he should remain there until he recovered sufficiently for investigations to resume. As he regained consciousness, however, he began to realise that there was a way of escape so long as the hospital guards thought that he was still ill enough to be unable to leave his bed. For days he feigned semi-consciousness and one night, when his guard was absent, he crept from the ward to the lavatories and managed to climb out of the window.

He made his way across France with the help of French families loyal to the Resistance, and occasionally with the help of the Resistance movement itself, and in this way he reached Paris where his parents lived. Having stolen a bunch of flowers from a flower stall for his mother, he rang the front door bell of the flat, but he was so filthy and ragged that his mother, who had thought her son must be dead, hardly recognised him. He might easily have been traced and rearrested by the Germans, but the war was drawing to a close, so in the end all was well and he managed to return to England.

One of his uncles, who was running the family shipping business, had been killed in an air raid during the war, and the company had been hard hit by losses at sea, so HL, at a very young age, was put in charge of the shipping company. Things did not go well and sadly the business was closed down soon after the war. HL felt that he was blamed by his family, and he was determined to redeem himself in their eyes.

It was long after this that I met him, but my war years having been in MI5, we got along well. Our friendship developed even more swiftly when HL discovered that we had a mutual interest in EHE, and more particularly in dreams, the meanings of which interested him enormously. While HL was regularly visiting his aunt Dorothy I was able to see him fairly often, but soon he went to live in the Isle of Man, and when she died she left her house on the Strand to be turned into the Topsham Museum. I missed Dorothy a great deal and helped with the complicated arrangements of starting the Topsham Museum. Contact between HL and myself was not so easy now, but we corresponded copiously during the following years.

I went over to the Isle of Man to stay with HL on a number of occasions, and found the weeks there a complete change to my life at home. Our meals usually consisted of a huge rice pudding and a large joint of beef, cooked by him in advance of my arrival, and intended to last a week in order that cooking would not interrupt talking-time. Every meal was the same throughout the week, but as we never stopped talking this went unnoticed. This aspect of HL's house-keeping suited me very well, but some of the other arrangements in the house were not quite so easy.

The bathroom had large windows overlooking other houses and it was explained to me that, because there were no curtains, HL would have the first bath in the mornings in order to steam up the windows so that I could bathe in privacy! I suggested that I might look into the question of some sort of window covering, but was told that this was an unnecessary expense, so the matter was dropped. He was also strict about turning off the switch for the hot water after bathing and it fell to me, as second bather, to remember this. However, on investigating the cupboard in which the tank was kept, I found that there had never been an insulating jacket on the boiler in all the years he had owned the house. Amazed at this lack of economy when he was so parsimonious in every other respect, I went out and bought a bright red plastic jacket for the boiler in order to surprise him.

The following morning I turned off the switch as usual after my bath, but was subjected to a severe reprimand when HL found that the washing-up water was still hot at lunchtime. I assured him that the switch was off and suggested that he should look in the cupboard. He came back and said, "What is that extraordinary red eiderdown on the tank?" I upset him quite a lot by telling him how much money he had wasted over the years by not covering up the tank, and added that he now owed me £6.5O for the insulated jacket. He could not believe that I had thought of buying such a thing, but after that at least we always washed up in hot water at midday.

I had noticed hanging in the cupboard with the tank innumerable beautiful, expensive Savile Row suits, every one of which seemed to me to be the same size and very similar in colour. The truth was that he had not changed shape since his youth, but continued to order a new suit periodically. The flat also contained a magnificent library of valuable books which had come to him from his father. The furniture was reasonable, some of it beautiful, but he was not prepared to spend money on comforts. He had become extremely deaf and never realised how much effort his friends had to put into conversations with him. He used complicated hearing aids, which were slung about his person and fixed by the telephone, but he had come to loathe using the phone, and, to assist conversations, was concentrating on developing his skill at lip-reading. I found these visits tiring but I was aware of the loneliness his lack of hearing caused him, and I loved him in spite of, or perhaps because of, his quixotic nature.

Chapter 37

Correspondence with Henri Leopold

Correspondence between Henri Leopold and me was overwhelming. He was a copious letter-writer, often sending three letters a week and expecting immediate replies, for he used letters like conversation. He was fascinated by dreams and wanted to examine them in detail, both when we met and in our letters, but of course the letters are the only record of this. Each one tended to overlap the next owing to the quantity and the speed with which he read and replied to my letters, and his insistence that I should reply immediately to his.

One of the early letters I received from Henri Leopold showed his concern about the frightening nightmares I had been having for many years. In fact they were more than nightmares and can only be described as night terrors. He wrote to me on the 7th December 1980 from The Athenaeum, his club in London:

Dear Diana,

Have you stopped screaming in the middle of the night? If you do still, have you found anyone with whom you can talk about it?

I carried away disquiet last time I saw you. Dreams with content and pattern are less ominous. I hope that all is well and that past anxieties have melted into the lovely drawings seen through the window strewn all over your dining room table.

With deep affection,

Henri Leopold

P.S. I hope your daughter is as happy in her room overlooking the river as I would be!

I replied that for the moment I had stopped screaming in the night. It was at this time that I went to work for 'Crisis at Christmas'. When I returned home I found another letter from him at The Athenaeum, saying:

> Dear Diana,
>
> I am very sorry that I shall miss you on the 23rd and that I cannot sleep with you on the Mile End Road. Presumably this area is heavily chaperoned?
>
> I shall be back here from the Isle of Man on January 10th. Will you be in London on any week-day after that date, and, if so, would you care to have luncheon with me here at the Athenaeum?
>
> In the meantime please have a Merry Xmas in the Mile End Road.
>
> Love,
>
> Henri Leopold.

However, he was full of advice about what he thought of as my nightmares in his next letter, writing:

> It is worrying. You are so vague. It is not advisable just to drift in and out of screaming. The root cause should be located, eradicated and replaced by serenity.

I was not sure that HL had realised the difference between night terrors and nightmares. Night terrors are not just unremembered dreams, they are something out of this world. It was night terrors which had caused me to fall down the stairs on two occasions when, while sleeping, I had left my bed to locate the distant screams of lost children. I therefore sent him a copy of the notes I had made some time before, describing one of my experiences.

Night Terrors

As sleep overtakes me, my heart races towards the ceiling. It is pounding as loudly as the footsteps of an intruder on the stairs. Leaden coils anchor my limbs; a child screams distantly from the depths of a cupboard, starving, lost, dangerously close to death. I have gone from a place of safety into an unknown world leaving the child to die. I scream with the child's cries, the howling of a wild thing. I am trapped within a terror more terrible than any reality, containing more fear than a waking thought, buried in a sleep of death, and always the fading cries of the child calling, calling, calling.

The coils are loosed from my limbs, I can tear through the house, up the stairs, which melt behind me as I fall, cold with the ice of terror, hopelessly searching. If only the cry would sound again, I would find the cry and still it. I am the child and the calling. Fear walks with me. I am FEAR.

Waking will return before a closed door, a door with no key, a house with no address, in a town with no name, and still the child will be crying; unto fear will be added failure, failure to quell the crying which weakens in the distance, and I am cold. I find myself in the dark passages of an unknown house.

I can act, I can use the telephone and ring for help. I dial frantically all the numbers which spring into my mind. A friend will go to the house and find the child, it will be safe. A voice speaks out of the darkness and I wake. I am holding the phone, it says "You have dialled the wrong number, please try again!"

These night terrors haunted me for years. When staying with me one night, my fourteen-year-old grandchild, Tamsen, rushed down from her bedroom believing that I was being murdered. Her description of the sounds which were coming from me in my sleep was that they were like those of 'a strangled dinosaur,' and I think her bravery in coming to my assistance was remarkable.

The night-terrors came to an abrupt stop when I woke one morning convinced that they had had a purpose. I saw humanity saturated with fear, cosmic fear, which fed upon the fear in the minds of the people.

Such unexplained fear could not be dispersed unless experienced in its fullness. I saw fear as a barrier to the hope of the world, a contagious disease. It appeared to me that there were those on this earth whose contribution towards the elimination of cosmic fear required them to take in and experience this undefined fear in order to clear the way towards peace.

My night terrors ceased after I had been given this explanation.

Chapter 38

Dreams

Having discovered Henri Leopold's interest in the interpretation of dreams, I found and sent him a description I had written of a dream which I had had some time before my divorce:

The Dream of a Great House

I was in a huge house filled with rowdy people. My husband, Robert, was there. He was asked to sign a paper permitting some of the people to throw the furniture out of the windows. He agreed and left.

I stood in the salon with a little boy. I knew that I must get him out of the house before he was harmed. He did not want to come. I carried a bucket of sand outside for him to play with and found that there was no garden, only a beach. (Coals to Newcastle!)

It was dark, and looking up at the house I could see Robert's brother, Ted, wearing a Viking's helmet, brandishing a large knife. He was with many other men who were also armed. They set the house on fire and threw the furniture from the windows. I realised that the furniture being thrown out was mine, and my bed fell from a window in the shape of a piece of corrugated iron. I tried to get back into the house to stop them. The doors were locked and I had to climb up the front of the building to get in. As I shouted at them they began to drift away and, still dreaming, I found myself outside my own house in Topsham running down the street to get help.

Henri Leopold's reply was prompt and to the point. He thanked me for the dream and went on to say:

Like the mathematician who took his dying colleague a number, you could not have chosen a better gift. You must be glad to have broken the sequence of violent awakenings from unremembered dreams.

Why do you think this one is self-explanatory? Are there not both alternative meanings and layers of meanings? I must not suggest, but here is one example taken from what you were saying a few days ago. Then you appeared to think of R., and one woman in particular, as no longer objective causes outside yourself, since you had, to a great extent, been successful in removing them from your life, and looked on them more as residuary problems inside your own attitudes and responses. In your letter you say that R. left during the dream and was not there when it all happened. Might it not be that he is not present in this house, which is yourself at the moment, because you have eliminated him as an active ingredient and are in fact doing all this to yourself?

If this interpretation is valid, and the house represents yourself and what is happening at this very moment, then your brother-in-law would only have provided the symbolic material quarried out of your memory with which to construct the dream. The destruction of the former contents of yourself, has now lit a fire which you cannot stop or even reach through locked doors.

This explanation rang true to me, but I had not been sufficiently educated in dream interpretation to work it out for myself. He finished his letter by asking whether I had ever heard Freud's comment that dreams were like sand - in view of the fact that the whole of this dream was surrounded by a beach and I was taking buckets of sand outside for the child to play with - but sadly, I have not been able to locate this quotation.

I followed up this dream by sending a description of another, more recent dream which contains far-reaching material which amazed me when I typed it into my computer. In this case I was unable to find any past experiences which would have supplied the source of the dream.

The Goat Dream

I was walking along a path which was narrow and rough. I was not afraid of the enormous drop upon the right-hand side, even though it was not possible to see to the bottom of the chasm where mists swirled, rising and receding like waves against a cliff face. The only indication that this was a dream came from the fact that there was no sound. The silence of dreams makes the content more potent, for we cannot break the barrier of noiselessness, and if it becomes necessary to scream, we are pulled from the womb of the dream, as in a traumatic birth with forceps clamped upon us, denying us the right to eject from the place of terror in our own time. On this occasion there was little indication of the night terrors to which I had become accustomed.

To my left fields spread out unhedged, green and flowered with daisies, poppies and flax. The grass was soft and tempting but I went forward on the path. Sunlight caught the shape of something unexpected in the middle of the field to my left. It seemed that a golden throne had been set up, on which sat a crowned figure. It was too distant to make out the details, but there was no doubt in my mind that it was a vision of Christ. I left the path and hurried across the field towards the vision, fearing that it would disappear as suddenly as it had materialised. As I came closer I was able to see that the apparition was clothed in a purple cloak and crowned with a three-pointed, medieval golden crown. The phrase "high and lifted up" crossed my mind and I hesitated. The figure turned to look over his shoulder at me and as he did so the whole contraption upon which he sat turned as if on a swivel, and I saw him for the first time for what he was, a remarkably human, bewhiskered goat, seated upon an upturned brass bedstead.

At the sight of me the goat went into paroxysms of silent laughter; he waved his hands in the air and laughed until his crown tilted over one eye, and the bed rocked backwards and forwards until it seemed certain to fall. It was some time later that I took in the fact that his fore feet were human hands, yet his hind feet were goatlike hooves. His face looked suspiciously like the actor, Peter O'Toole. It was the sudden reversal of all that I had expected which made me step backwards, but I was not afraid. He seemed delighted that his trick had worked so well, and it took me a while to realise that he was a chimera, a whimsical, play-acting afflatus, the trickster, who would disappear as soon as I ceased to believe in him. I returned to the path, now shrouded in mist from the chasm below. I could neither see my feet nor the edge of the cliff and there was danger in every step.

I wondered if this apparition was in fact the great god Pan of whom, in the past, I had been rather fond. Or was it the Devil, in which case he was confirming the existence of God, for I thought that the Devil could not exist in the absence of God.

As I expected, I received a long letter from HL in reply to this dream, in the course of which he wrote:

> *You have the most natural gift for activating archetypes coupled with what seems to me a refusal to accept their message. What difficulty does your conscious have in accepting what your unconscious formulated so clearly?*

> *The devil could not exist without God any more than wrong without right or left without right. The negative infers the positive, destruction without creation really is putting the cart before the horse.*

> *So you see the archetypal goat with a crown on his head and your wisdom travels at one jump the road that took Huysmans three books and many years; who, when seeing the power achieved by Satanists when desecrating the host in the black mass, realised that the host could not be a figment, and ended his life as a Benedictine. Yet when you wake up you can no longer understand the logic of the argument. However, you do notice that the left hand way is not for you and that your road is the straight (and narrow?) one which leads on to the right true end.*

> *All your symbols are so clear. You seem to me close to integration, but unwilling to take the last step.*

> *Your sketch of the crowned goat was extraordinary.*

HL came down to Topsham the following weekend. I saw him approaching down the Strand as dusk fell on the town, his Inverness cape blowing out behind him in the wind. When he reached my house, he deposited a large tome on my hall table and said that he would be back that evening to discuss it.

The book turned out to be a French history of black magic! My French not being equal to it, I was not able to read any of the book before his return that evening. When he arrived later he found a page on which was an ancient black-and-white print of a crowned goat on a pedestal. The remarkable thing, as far as I was concerned, was that it had human hands, just as my goat had had, and was also crowned with a three-pointed crown.

HL assured me that the goat in my dream was too much of a coincidence and that I must, at some time, have had recourse to books on black magic where I would have seen this print, and that this was why I had used it in my dream. I was absolutely certain that I had not seen the print before. I had not the slightest difficulty in accepting that such a symbol could have arrived in my dream from some mystic source, to be used for a very 'non-black magic' purpose. What we neither of us thought about at the time was the possibility of precognition! It seems so obvious to me now that the very act of HL bringing down the book for me to see, after the event, had enabled the identical goat to appear in my dream. My goat was benign, and in fact I have become rather fond of him. He showed me that I must have a care about running off at a tangent in search of unknown gods: the dream ended by a return to the narrow path which I had been following before the diversion.

My experience of precognition in dreams had already been shown vividly in the dream of meeting the woman on the railway station, which I had had while married to Robert. There are three factors which must be adhered to in confirming all precognitive experiences, the first being that the dream or experience is expressed in writing, or at least verbally, in advance of the event. The second is that the detail in the dream or experience must be sufficient to enable the event to be recognised, and the third is that all other explanations for the experience, such as auto-suggestion, telepathy etc. must be able to be ruled out. The detail in this dream and the outcome resulting from it are sufficient to meet all of these factors.

Time passed and my habit of calling Henri Leopold 'HL' changed over the years into a habit we both developed of referring to each other as 'Guardian' or just 'G'. At the time I said to him that this was going to make it hard for anyone who might have to decipher our letters in the distant future.

A Sonnet to Love

If God is Love, and I have love for you,
then, when I hold your hand, or let my lips
stray round your sleeping eyes, I give you God;
and when some evenings you stride down my street
in haste to leave the claustrophobic train,
your cloak stretched from your shoulders in the wind
and head bowed down to meet the falling rain,
I would strew love like petals at your feet -
a love which suchtimes calls my heart to stop
and start again with sudden stabs of pain.
For so I love you, dearest, yet I know
that where your life is led I may not go.
So must I keep these memories with me
in some safe place where you and I can be.

Chapter 39

Two More Dreams

Many letters passed between us as 'Guardians' throughout the following years, one of which from me included the following:

The Dream of The Red Temple

When the dream began I was in a modern house in which were a number of society women and a few men. The voices of the women were high-pitched and overpowering. They were dressed in the fashion of the 1920's: drop-waisted dresses with short skirts, cloche hats and long cigarette holders. Most of them were smoking. I could not fit in with them socially, and their gossip irritated me. I felt that they were friends of the man with whom I had come to the party and I began to think that we were not suited to each other.

In the dream I left the room and went out across a field. Someone, perhaps the man mentioned above, joined me when I went out and at some point we seemed to merge our thoughts; I was aware of his presence but I could not see him.

Bright sunlight was falling on the walls of a building which I could see floating above the earth, far off above a wide expanse of arid desert. It glowed as red as "a rose-red city half as old as Time," and we moved towards it as if magnetised.

As we approached, the building materialised into a great, circular, red-walled Temple. Its domed roof, being of copper, reflected the brilliance of the sun, and I saw the building suspended above the earth as if floating within a mirage. There were many doors in the surrounding walls, through one of which I passed into the interior. The floor of the circular Temple was laid out formally with streams of water forming paths, and every path led towards the centre. The shallow paths were bounded on each side by low stone walls, three or four inches in height, dividing the area into a geometric pattern, a mandala. I cannot recall exactly what plants filled the triangles between the paths, but they seemed to be low-growing herbs forming a vast conservatory, a place of growth.

I followed a stream into the Temple, the water lapping crystal clear and cool about my feet. At the centre was a circle of stone. The wall was waist-high and I approached expecting to find a pool fed by the streams of water. All was still and peaceful and I was not prepared for the shock which was to come. Leaning over the wall to look down into the water I was thrown back in fear, for I was looking into the dark night of Eternity.

I had entered the Temple in sunlight but now I was alone with the night sky spread out below me. I could see through it to a depth of stars. Turning my eyes to the golden dome above me I could discern a further open circle through which I saw the same dark night of Eternity above me as below. My fear grew. The Temple, designed by my dream, now seemed to me as a trap floating alone in Eternity. I saw it as my self, the many doors and paths all representing choices to be made in the course of my life, and yet all leading to the centre, the Eternity from which there was no escape.

The dream was a profound experience.

This dream resulted in a series of letters between HL and me as 'Guardians', and some discussions which I have not included here. One letter of mine said that I had realised from his previous letter that I had *"not given sufficient importance to the indication of growth which is shown in the dream"*. It also referred to a question which he had posed me - *"Why are you afraid of the eternity which awaits you?"* - to which I replied that this would need a lot of thought.

Soon after this we met in the Isle of Man and continued our discussion on these deeply involved questions. Recently I found the following notes, which were an attempt to answer his question:

In reply to your question on what you see as my fear of eternity, the simplest answer would be physical death, but I am not afraid of death. I do not think of it in any way connected with the

termination of ourselves which we may sometimes experience in
dreams. However, it is necessary to rethink such a point as this
again and again because this vision of eternity is not a physical
experience, as it would be if one really went up to the wall of a
well and looked into eternity. It is a growth of knowledge which
is put before us in dreams because, being human, we do not want to
face such an impossible subject.

In reply to your comment, "when you are faced with the well of
eternity your library will be locked away from you and you will
not be allowed that way out. No escapism could be permitted, it
will be you, not your library which will supply the answers!"
This seems to me to be more a problem for you than for me: I have
no library and yours is vast. For either of us it would be a giant
step to take to jump over the wall of the well and into eternity.
This would take terrifying courage should such a demand be
made. We would have to have reached the point where our faith
had become strong enough.

There is a very close association between this dream and the
earliest dream that I can recall. I do not think that we have
discussed this particular one as it occurred long before I met you.
If you would like to have a copy I will send it to you.

The result was that Henri Leopold asked for this dream to be sent
to him. It was a dream that I had had when I was in Africa, at our
cottage in the mountains, shortly after the Inyanga experience. That
area was a psychic place where one might expect such 'big dreams' to
occur.

The White Robed Circle

As I slept I became the Watcher in my dream, and I lay in the
cool depths of a round, stone-built pool in a strange country. In
spite of knowing myself to be under the water, I was still able
to see into the distance. A column of white-robed Beings left a
far-off, whitewashed city and moved like a frieze carved in
stone on the walls of an ancient temple; progressing slowly they
circled a baize-green painted lawn which stretched across the
landscape. Each figure kept its space, looking neither to right
nor left but following the Leader, their white cowls hiding their

faces. The Leader seemed to gather life from the sunlight, and as he drew closer he was set apart from his followers. They moved like effigies, replicas of their former selves, but he traversed the land with serenity and purpose.

All was silent. Even the water in the pool was not, as yet, disturbed by his coming. Only the Watcher in the darkness of the water felt the thrill of his presence and lifted herself towards the light. The reflection of the face of the Leader lay upon the surface of the water, and the Watcher, who was only one of the Earth's smallest creatures, was seized with a great desire to approach this Being; yet she hid herself in fear as the followers arrived and circled the stone walls of the pool. The heat of the day drummed upon the Earth, while the shining figures floated above the water in a haze, their reflections transforming the pool with the whiteness of their clothing. The Watcher, cowering under the surface weeds, saw herself for the first time for what she was, a tiny black, microscopic creature.

Suddenly the surface of the water was broken and the Leader gathered her up. She lay in the palm of his hand, apprehensive, stranded, small and black. As his eyes fell upon her she was turned instantly into gold. For one brief moment she saw his face before he returned her to the pool, where she sped across the surface of the water celebrating her joy. She had been held in the hand of Love and had been transformed.

When I woke from this dream it was as if a transformation had occurred within myself, as if he, the Great Alchemist, had changed the base metal of my being within the crucible of his hand. Somehow I knew that the heat required for this change had been derived from suffering, which had been endured and which I would continue to endure in the future. Great experiences are gifted to us in advance, at a time when we have no knowledge that there will be any payment required for the blessings received. Equally, if it was known that suffering would, one day, open a path to joy, we would not experience the full effect of the pain. The whole of every experience must be included into our life's pattern here on this planet. I have no comments from HL on this dream, although I recall that we mentioned it. Perhaps it was too 'big' for me to permit discussion.

HL was always keen that I should join the Roman Catholic Church, where he was sure I would find the security for which I was searching. I had fallen away from my belief in the Anglican Church (though not my belief in Christ) for reasons which would have applied equally well to the Roman Catholic church, and was determined not to fall out of the frying pan into the fire. I was deeply distrustful of the word 'religion', which seemed to me to denote membership of a club, rather than a spiritual search for Truth, but HL asked how I could know this until I had experienced the Mass in a Roman Catholic church. For him this was *his* search for Truth, but to me it seems that his church required adherence to certain rules and man-made dogmas which were not my way to Truth. We agreed to differ, but he remained concerned for my future.

Chapter 40

Concern for Henri Leopold

Towards the end of 1992 HL and I had the chance to talk seriously on the subject of dying and I could tell that he was personally worried about it. His letters now seemed sad and I was concerned for him. He wrote to me about an Open Mind Group which I had been running for some time:

> *Thank you very much for your letter. It is the one thing that has cheered me up in an otherwise troubled scene.*
>
> *I am so glad that you have given me a list of your Group members. It is much easier to visualise now. How excellent to have started one that is joined by university professors in the hope of widening their knowledge. You tell me that James is succeeding quite well. I would give a lot to be present at one, it sounds such a good mixture. Two Quakers, a Theosophist, the semi-Buddhist, James and you present a wide range of approaches. Would you accept the addition of a Roman Catholic if I were in Topsham? The widow, the sky meditator and James are all indispensable and spread out to offer variety. Besides some, like James, appear in both categories - or perhaps I should say all. The whole point and secret of a successful group is to awaken the Janus in ourselves, since we not only face both ways, but do so in every aspect.*
>
> *The Sufi awaiting a gap in which to join seems too close to the denominations already present for perfection. Sufis are outside the main structure of Islam, Quakers are outside all structures, Theosophists claim to unite all structures, the semi-Buddhist is presumably semi and you and James are not main-stream Christians. (?) What you need is a pillar of the Church, such as me, to present total orthodoxy, in his own eyes.*

Towards the end of the year HL seemed to lose his ability to write with an open mind; it seemed to me that he was trying to regain his lost belief in the Roman Catholic doctrines in which he had been brought up.

It was at this point that I received a letter from him which was deeply worrying. He wanted to know my opinion about purgatory, in detail. Sadly, that letter is lost and I cannot include it here, but I have my reply which was written towards the end of March 1993.

Dearest G,

This letter is probably the last I shall write to you until May. I am so involved with Easter holidays and the family, and then go to Schumacher College until the 25th April.

Perhaps during this lull you could read The Coming of the Cosmic Christ *by Matthew Fox (a fellow RC). It might help you to understand much of what I think. I picked up the book the other day on impulse (never reject your impulses!) and it puts into words so many of the things I am trying to explain. Perhaps one of the real difficulties is that I believe in reincarnation and you probably don't. I doubt if Matthew Fox does either, but that I shall shortly find out at Schumacher.*

The reason for referring to Christ as Cosmic is to return Him to the rest of the world after years when the churches have kept Him apart. For me the Christ IS Cosmic, He is Everything. I may have told you of one visualisation which I had some years ago which seemed to help me to understand the Cosmic nature of Christ.

> I was a primitive woman, dying in labour giving birth to a child, and hoping that it would die like the rest of my children. Outside the mud hovel in which I lived were three graves, symbols of three dead children. The man in my life was a violent, primitive, evil being. As the contractions grew stronger I felt the power within me pushing me up through the earth, as a plant or tree forces itself towards the light. Breaking through the Earth's crust I saw myself as a flower opening into the sunlight in a field of flowers. I turned towards the sun and knew that I had been reborn.

Dreams come up sometimes in the Group, usually started by me, as most people feel that any dream they have has no meaning and is not important. I hope to help them to realise the importance of dreams in the way you have taught me. I owe you so much for your help. My concept of a Guardian has not changed: it has widened perhaps. I love you as much for our disagreements as for our agreements!

You ask me what I believe about purgatory. I don't believe in it as a 'place', of course, only as a state of mind. If you die convinced that you will be punished, tortured, because of the life you have led, you may initially find you have made a new life for yourself which appears to you in this way, but where is Love? Where is forgiveness? This state in which you imagine yourself to be is not the state which Love has in mind for you. Your church and mine so often seem to forget that God IS Love. Doctrines and dogma have little to do with the depths of love which will be shown to you in your new life. Forget them and remember only that which you personally believe in and have searched for; that is what you will find. The last sentence in your letter sounds sad. Dare I ask you what the blocks and barriers are which you mention? If you write I will answer before I leave.

I love you, but you know that, and you will always be a Guardian to me as I hope to remain a Guardian to you.

Chapter 41

The Death of Henri Leopold

Notes made on 1st April 1993, on learning of the death of HL.

Was it prophetic that in that letter to Henri Leopold I began by saying, "This may be the last letter I shall write to you"?

Henri Leopold was found dead on the stairs of his house this evening. I have prayed that he died instantly without pain. I had been concerned for him over the past weeks, as he did not seem to me to be in his usual positive frame of mind. My distress at his going is beyond words, and I must leave him to record his last moments, as he did, in his own way.

An account by Henri Leopold of his last night on earth:

Thursday, April 1st, 1993
6.55 a.m.

I woke at three o'clock with a pain in my chest, after a time managed to get down to All Bran, returned to coffee in bed thinking I would not be able to take the dogs for their walk, fell asleep and had unusual dream, after which pain gone, dressed slowly, drove to golf course, as walk started pain returned and got worse and worse each time uphill, made it slowly to car, dogs very sympathetic, back in bed with pain continuing.

Dream

I was in bed here, but in a bleak white room with bare electric light bulb and nothing on walls, in a spartan hotel bed littered with sheets, covered in my hand-writing. I talked on the telephone to Jean Francois Rousseau (which I have never done) in French (which I never do) about a number of subjects which had no significance...........

Through the half open door of the bedroom I saw my father and mother pass separately in their night clothes. I hoped that my father heard me speaking French as this would make him happy.

A distant person with whom I was on formal unfriendly terms came into the room and started to take off the top half of her nightwear. This surprised me. She turned shyly away from me and I looked down so as not to embarrass her. But then she turned towards me. I looked up and saw, splashed across the underside of her breasts, a streak of very light transparent water-colour blue. I wondered at the time, "Why blue? Why paint?" The breasts were charmingly rounded like those of a statue and had not begun to sag.

I have never dreamt of J. F. R. before and all the elements of this part, except the last, are unlikely. I often dream of my father nowadays. The girl I can associate with the present transition state between staring at and abstaining from staring (not wanting to stare?) at girls. It is already no more than a lingering misconnection of desire for the absolute...

Blue is the colour of Mary, who has been in my thoughts lately in connection with Catholicism being the right religion for feminists. The paleness of the colour may be a symbol of the inappropriate context - unless they are bringing me to her for a deeper purpose.

The bareness of the room may suggest that I should recover the French part of myself and my family memories and true faith, freed from distractions, not through the books, pictures, tapestries, furniture from the past that cocoon me here, but with a fresh start that braves the telephone [which he could not use because of his deafness] *for the sake of maintaining social contacts, however desultory, and retain only the writing as an essential that covers the bed...*

After forty-five minutes recording this the pain is less.

Those paragraphs were written by HL early on the morning of his death. Afterwards he had a bath, and was found at five o'clock that evening lying dead. It was the friend who found him who very kindly sent me a copy of Henri Leopold's last note.

I think, thank God, that HL's death must have been instant, for he was still holding his towel and soap. He died alone, as he had lived for the last part of his life. We had discussed the fact that this would be so, but neither of us had realised that it would be so sudden and without warning to anyone. His account does not indicate that he thought that his death was imminent, just that he was concerned and worried. He had never mentioned to me that his heart was playing up, but that was his way: he only very rarely mentioned his health.

Elegy

Earth-hard the grave dug on a barren hill,
stream-watered, set in rock.
You were that rock;
you also were the stream
I loved to follow saving your words,
your thoughts, your argument,
climbing with you the paths
of your profound discourse
and passionate conviction.

 All gone.

The gate is closed against your journeying,
the path without your footprints
disappears - reverts - uncharted.
Tear-blinded to the sanctity of hills,
holding the cold stone faces of the rocks,
which guard the ancient graveyards of the earth,
I pour my small libation on the stones.

Dark Memories

Once when I climbed the disused staircase of your life
and stood before closed doors,
I watched them open on the dust of half-lit rooms,
and I, amazed, stood still.
Beyond each open door within your life,
I found revealed the secrets of your past;
one room was filled with childhood toys,
but many more were carpeted with fear
from days, long gone, in France;
recalling prison bars and endless hours
of tortured pain on bloodstained, cold stone floors
in white-tiled passages, furnished with ropes
and sharp, steel implements, in basement chambers,
deep below the distant sounding surface of the street.

I took a brush and swiftly painted out such memories,
and drew your spirit in towards the light,
which slipped between the shredded curtain-folds
and streaked the carpets, faded under dust.
One room there was where treasured books
guarded the house with many thousand words,
and in the watered sunlight I could see
the movement of your hands between the shelves;
they wandered lovingly, blessing each volume
which had stood its ground, in spite of evil
in a brain-washed world.
Then climbing up towards the attic floor,
you turned and smiled at me, and raised your hand,
and entered into that small sanctuary
where you, in youthful years, had found your peace.

Chapter 42

James Smeall

In 1984 James Smeall had become a good friend. We met through Alan Milton who had been a friend of mine in Rhodesia, and at whose suggestion I had come to Topsham to buy a house in 1971. Alan Milton had lived for many years at White House in Ebford, near Topsham, and James Smeall, who had a house in Topsham, was a close friend of his.

When Alan retired, James Smeall also retired and came from Exeter to live in his Topsham house. He was very well known and had held various important posts in his life, being head of St. Luke's College in Exeter from the end of the war, and later Mayor of Exeter. He took over St. Luke's when it had been seriously damaged by bombs, rebuilt it and, at the same time, rebuilt its reputation as a teacher training college. He has always been remembered with great affection by his students.

During the first few years that Robert and I were in Topsham we did not get to know James and his wife very well, but when Alan Milton came to stay with us from Africa, James came to our house to meet up with him again. It was only after my divorce and the death of James' wife in 1984 that I really became friendly with him. By that time both James and I were alone.

James walked past my house one morning when I was outside, and stopped and asked if I knew that his wife had died. I had just returned from America and had not heard of her death. He looked so ill that I asked him in for coffee and he stayed for a long time as he needed to talk.

From that time onwards James walked down to my house frequently and we became close friends. He was a man of great charm, an excellent conversationalist with an enormous sense of humour. It took some time before I realised all this, for at first James was exhausted from nursing his wife through a long and depressing illness until her death in the spring. By the summer of that year, however, he began to look a different person. James was renowned in Topsham for his ability to entertain with both interesting and diverting stories and he was loved by everyone who knew him.

The house that James had built, 'Follett Orchard', was on high ground within the town and had a wonderful view of the distant hills and the Exe estuary. His garden was his joy and he never ceased to work in it. In his absent-minded way he left numerous articles of clothing, and particularly his spectacles, hanging on bushes in different parts of the garden. The clothing was not hard to find, but the spectacles might remain blossoming on plants from one season to another; he was always having to replace them.

The house itself was strangely built, a 'prefab' fixed securely on the roof of a concrete platform. Underneath was storage space in which he housed the car, and various useful areas where other things could be kept. He lived above in a two bedroomed flat with two bathrooms, a sitting room, a kitchen and a balcony overlooking the river, and he was very proud of having the best view in Topsham.

James did not get to know HL very well because soon after my meeting with him, HL went to live in the Isle of Man. They were very different, and I found the variations in their interests fascinating. They had both been at Cambridge University before the war but James had left before HL arrived. I do not think that they would ever have become great friends as they would probably have competed with each other. They were both great debaters and between them they filled the spaces in my life. I valued their friendships for many years.

Both James and I had houses in Topsham which we dearly loved and we did not want to leave them. I valued my privacy and my tiny riverside garden, and he loved his view of the river and his large garden. I was happy with things as they were and we lived 'semi-detached' for many years, taking our holidays together and meeting almost every day. However, there came a time when James really wanted us to get married. He was tired of living on his own and I could see that he would have liked to have me with him all the time. I was happy to keep things as they were, however. I had a large family and did not want to overburden him with them. His house was not at all suitable for my family reunions and I did not think that his own family would have taken kindly to such a development in our relationship. My children were all very fond of him and would have had no objections to such an arrangement, but I saw no advantage in changing the way we were.

As we grew older and health problems arose, I could, and did, go over to his house to stay and look after him at different periods, and we took our holidays together up until the final year of his life. We were very close to each other, and I value his love deeply.

"We are Diana's foresters - minions of the Moon"

Henry 1V Part 1

The lunatic, the lover and the poet
Follow the moon,
I am not yet lunatic
My attic
Harbours the growing rat
Not yet the bat
Who will come all too soon.
And as a lover
My moonlight nights are over
For visiting Endymion out of time,
But words I have to breathe autumnal passion
I am your minion, dear Diana, in my fashion.

James Smeall

Chapter 43

Contact with Mediums

I had never thought of contacting a medium until a friend of mine made an appointment for me to see a clairvoyant who was visiting in Exeter. His name was George Pratt and he had a remarkable reputation. I was not at all sure what to expect but, having been told that I would not be wasting his time, I made my way to the appointment. I brought a blank audio tape with me, as he expected to record the meeting. I found him to be a gifted and kindly man.

We sat and talked for a short while and he then told me that I had three guides, one of whom was an Indian 'whose stature is his knowledge.' He explained that where we have no earthly bodies 'our stature' is determined by our knowledge. I did not take in the significance of this at the time, but in the light of subsequent experiences, in the company of other mediums, it has become clear. Knowledge of the right sort, spiritual wisdom, or what I would prefer to call 'knowing', gained in the course of a life, depicts our stature within the next dimension beyond death. I am grateful to George for this simple way of expressing the unimaginable, for it has helped me to see that the Mind/Wisdom which moves with us into Spirit forms the stature of our new being by which we will be recognised.

George asked why he was being shown a particular sea shell about which there was a story. This was remarkable as the shell was one which I had found on Holy Island some years before and which, at the time, I had recognised as being 'given' to me by Hugh; throughout the following years it had become a talisman for me. Strangely, at that particular moment with George I could not recall it, perhaps because it had ceased to be a sea shell in my mind. On my return home I found it lying on top of all the things in my untidy dressing-table drawer, to which position it must have been moved as it normally lay in its own box.

George told me that I was a counsellor, to which I replied that I was not a qualified counsellor, and he said, "in the eyes of the right Being you are a counsellor." He began to have a feeling of discomfort in his throat and said, "I don't like the feeling, cancer or something like that." He asked me if there was anyone in Spirit who might have died in this way. I felt sure that it must be Ted, whose death I have described earlier. Cancer had perforated his heart and he had died of a massive haemorrhage. George felt that this was right as he was also feeling a connection with the heart. He said that he associated Ted with the great purple healing colour which was surrounding me; he was very insistent that there was a great cloud of healing surrounding Ted and myself at the time of his death.

At this point a man came forward, and George asked if I knew who he was. I told him that it was likely to be my fiancé. He saw great warmth and fondness between us which would always be there. George was given the name David to pass on to me, and said I would discover why. Later I realised that the connection must be the saving of David from drowning many years before, when I had known that my actions were controlled by some other Being or power.

Some time later I was handed an audio tape-recording which had been made at a session at which George had been the medium. Towards the end of the evening it was thought by those present that George was emerging from the trance through which he had been speaking, but instead he began to speak in a new voice. One or two people wondered who it was, who was about to speak.

What follows on the tape sent shivers down my spine when I first heard it, for I recognised the meaning of the words coming from George as being identical to the meaning of those which had been placed in my mind many years before on the mountain in Africa. He spoke in a strange voice, quiet yet penetrating, slowly but with enormous conviction:

Even now you ask "Who is this?"
Know, accept, feel and accept.

I am the breath in the morning,
I am the lull in the night.
I am that which comes
as it was said I would come,
and I will be known by those who know me
but I shall not be known by strangers.
Yet that which I give I must give to all.

I am the dawn and the sunset,

I am the sun and the stars.

I am Love.

I am Love.

I am Love.

His final words faded to a faint whisper.

I wrote to George and sent him a copy of this transcript, to which he replied thanking me and telling me that he had never heard it himself. He again spoke of the importance of counselling as being, in many cases, more relevant than healing and went on to say:

> You know, the co-operation of the sitter is much more important than is realised in bringing about a good communication, so you played as great a part as I in our sitting.

Soon after this George died and so I was never able to meet him again. He had given me so much more than I write here, most of it deeply personal.

Dorothy Chitty

It it was a long while before I could bring myself to meet a medium or a clairvoyant again. I did not want the world to see the loss and pain which had haunted me through the years, and yet I also knew that I could no longer suppress the truth I had been given. Eventually I agreed to meet a medium called Dorothy Chitty who had been recommended to me.

We had a short discussion during which she told me that she did not want to hear any details of why I had come to see her. She found it much more convincing if she was able to speak as she heard within her mind, without her own thoughts getting in the way. As we sat together she suddenly broke off our conversation and switched on her tape-recorder. She started to speak at once to an unknown Being who was trying to bring all three of us together, someone known to me but not to Dorothy. She said that she could see him so close to me that he was nearly part of me, and believed himself to be my husband.

Shaking with the tension I felt at the approach of this Being, I dared not believe who it was. To reach out to the truth I asked her to ask how he had died. Dorothy appeared to be nonplussed by this and asked how it was that I did not know. I did not reply to this because it was important that I did not tell her anything about him, or who he was. It could have influenced my trust in her words.

The following is taken directly from the audio tape which was made at the time:

> A scar is healing. He has been around all the time, he is the cover for the pages in between. He is showing me space around him, above and below, he says that just before he died he was laughing with his friends.
>
> It was very quick, he did not suffer, instantaneous. I feel as though my head is expanding - a violent end. He was not shot in the head - a sort of explosion.

To Dorothy this did not make sense. How could he have been in space with his friends? I told her that Hugh and his crew were 'missing' in the Battle of Britain over the English Channel in 1940. It was the greatest relief to me to know that their deaths were instantaneous.

The circumstances of Hugh's dying having been known to no-one, not even me, I was amazed that Dorothy could have seen it all so clearly. When contacted later, Hugh's sister said that those in authority at the time had thought that he might possibly have been shot down in error by a British destroyer, but if this was so it had never been publicly acknowledged by the authorities. I had not been told as Hugh's family had thought it would add to my distress.

Because of Hugh's extraordinary revelations through Dorothy Chitty, I continued to go to see her when I felt compelled to do so and, as with this first meeting, all the following accounts were recorded on audio tape in order that I could keep them for reference in the future.

At the next meeting Dorothy started by telling me that I had always known that I was 'a chosen child' and that I had been gifted with mediumship and had been given ancient wisdom. She asked who Jon was, and said that from the past, and towards the future, someone was calling his name. This was so unexpected that I found myself close to tears. Jon is the name of my Downe's Syndrome grandson who has never been able to speak. He has grown to be a man, affectionate, musical and a painter. I would love to have known who was calling him, for it seemed to indicate that someone was caring for him from another world.

Dorothy went on to say that there was a man standing beside me who had a great deal of love towards me.

> He is giving you an olive branch and a rose, from him to you,
> to take you into the future. He is a teacher, a lovely man. He
> is tapping something. He is making a tapping sound.

At first I was unable to place the noise of tapping, but suddenly it came to me that the sound was being made by a man called Norman Yendell to disclose to me who he was. He had been a sculptor in olive wood. I should have known at once when he gave me the olive wood! Norman was truly a 'lovely man' and was a great friend and guide. I had frequently been to his house in Longdown in Devon to talk with him.

Not long before my meeting with Dorothy I had left for a holiday in America and had particularly asked Norman not to die while I was away! I don't know what made me say this, but Norman had smiled and said he would try not to. However, he had died alone in his little house before my return. He was not found for several days, but from the description of how he was found he must have died instantly: he still had his eleven o'clock biscuit in his hand and his coffee was on the table close to where he lay. Norman was a saintly man and I am deeply grateful for his friendship.

The Flying Officer

As the shot swan, when
he in feathered flakes
drifted towards the sea
and settled there,

brief moments,
while the waves washed
clean that which had held
his spirit in the light;

and all that flying beauty
sank into darkness,
leaving soul to wander
on the surface of the
might-have-been.

Then, gathering the loving
which had made his life,
he flew his spirit down
the bright lit path, across
the world towards the
setting sun.

Written for Hugh Haswell as a result of hearing the details of his death.

Chapter 44

Dorothy and the Return of Jean

A few months later, in 1991, my aunt Molly's oldest daughter, my cousin Jean (who had married the younger brother of P. K. Van der Byl) died in Johannesburg. Her sisters, Anne Lorentz and Elizabeth Smith, knowing that I had contact with a clairvoyant, wrote to ask me if I could get in touch with Dorothy to find out whether Jean was safe. I managed to get an appointment quite soon, which in itself was strange because Dorothy is usually very booked up, and the circumstances of Jean's death were so unusual that I did not want to discuss any of it with Dorothy in advance. However, during the session Dorothy suddenly said that she was feeling restrictions in her throat and that someone with a lot of feeling was present. She thought it was a woman who had not been dead for very long and was finding it hard to communicate. I asked her to find out how this person had died, as I wanted to identify her.

Dorothy: I don't know how long she has been over but it is quite close. I feel as if I want to cry - distress. She is taking me to long grass, pain of the heart. She is backing away, it is getting darker. I feel a cloak, she is underneath it - panic, I feel panicky. I am scared - can't speak.

I don't know what this is about but it is a bit scary in here. Running away. She is running away - can't speak. I feel as though I am running away. I am starting to shake.

Here I intervened. I knew that it must be Jean, because Jean had been murdered. I did not feel it was fair to Dorothy to allow it to go on any longer, for she was becoming really frightened. I told her that Jean had been killed.

Dorothy: Ah, no pain, no pain. She's all right now. I am standing looking around. I am looking down, confusion. Someone has given her a white rose. She is tapping you on the shoulder. She is desperate to make contact.

She is having tea, sandwiches, a fruit cake, on a table in the garden. She is showing us wild flowers. She is a very happy person.

She is telling us that when she died she was taken to a place of healing, a room with no walls. She wasn't sure where she was. There were many rooms. She says no pain, just a beginning. I have to tell you that this spirit has no face.

I asked whether Jean had any messages for her sisters and, through Dorothy, Jean said that she was holding them together. She went on to say that the loss of material things does not matter, the loss of life does not matter and the loss of love does not happen. Jean then proceeded to speak of some distressing family matters of which I knew nothing, but the important thing was that she had come through the murder and was on the way to recovery and was able to send love to her sisters.

The strangest thing that came out of the interview with Jean, and which convinced her sisters that it really was her, was something which I knew nothing about and felt was unimportant, and in fact nearly left out of my transcript altogether. This was the presence of a fruit cake on her tea-table! Both her sisters knew immediately that Jean had shown this symbol because it could only be understood by them, because it concerned a private joke between the three of them.

When Anne, the younger sister, had been seriously ill in America, Jean had told Elizabeth, the middle sister, that she had been so worried about Anne that she had eaten a whole fruit cake! When Anne recovered and returned home, they frequently teased Jean about this and recommended a fruit cake as a cure for worry and distress. That Jean had shown a fruit cake on her tea-table, and that it was apparently whole, showed them that she was not distressed, had not needed to eat any of it, and could even joke with them about it! I find it extraordinary that such a commonplace incident could have been so dramatically important in confirming to them that it was Jean herself speaking.

Again and again I have found that it is the easily-missed symbols which prove the presence of the Spirit of the person, and which give the most comfort to those who are grieving for them.

To those who might suspect that Dorothy was reading my mind during this interview, I have to say that I knew no details of Jean's death apart from the fact that she had been murdered. I had been banned from entering South Africa and consequently I had not seen any of my cousins for some years. I find it impossible to discover any alternative explanation to this detailed account and must accept it as direct clairvoyance in the presence of Jean herself.

In the following year I had another meeting with Dorothy. She told me that I would write a book and that it was important that I should get on with it.

She said:

> I also have to tell you of the death of a friend. You have a lot
> of love for him.

This, of course, referred to the death of HL which at the time of that particular meeting had not yet occurred. I dreaded the possibility that she was referring to him but had a premonition that this was so.

Chapter 45

The Return of HL

During the months following his death I was concerned for HL and deeply distressed that so much had been left unfinished. I made an appointment to see Dorothy Chitty in the autumn of that year. Dorothy had never met Henri Leopold nor did she know of him, or of our close friendship. Neither, of course, was she aware that he was the person whose death she had predicted some time before.

When I arrived at Dorothy's house I told her that a close friend of mine had died and that I wanted to contact him. She wondered how she was going to find him and I said that he would come if he wished to.

The following account is written as the interview came through on the tape at the time, with any gaps being those moments when Dorothy was trying to understand what was being shown to her. Dorothy is speaking with HL, and the words spoken directly between them are typed in italics.

Dorothy began:

> I have picked up the initial 'T'. I have to give it to you: it is for a man. I called in to Spirit and he said, "A man with the initial 'T' will find him for you.

I believe that 'T' was for my brother-in-law Ted, whom Henri Leopold had met and become fond of at the time when Ted was dying in my house a few years previously. He was the one most likely to respond to my call for Henri Leopold, but to my consternation, a few moments later, Dorothy said that there was a man coming towards me with his hands in chains! Then there was a pause, after which she said:

All I have now is a man saying he has no chains -"*Look no chains*" - as if he is surprised, as though he felt he ought to have chains -"*the chains I felt I had all my life.*"

They never were there but he felt that he had them and they are on his hands. He is saying, "*My experience while living was that I always had to have a reason for living, but the reason became the excuse.*" He feels he caused pain, unconscious pain. "*I went through a cleansing.*" While I am watching him it is as if he is standing under a waterfall, a waterfall of light. It is cleansing him, it went right through him.

"*Now I can speak.*" He has a lot to say this man; he is not very strong. "*Now I can be myself.*" He was never really himself in the body. There is something poetic about him - words. He is giving me a feeling of 'poetic'. "*At last I have found peace, peace of mind.*"

He knew his moment of death. He is saying, "*The day was appropriate, I had acted as a fool.*" [HL died on 1st April!] There is a lot of laughter with him. He is sending love to you, a great deal of love and thanking you, "*She was a shoulder to cry on, she was my healer.*"

Then turning from Dorothy to me, he said:

"*And in return I will help you with your words.*

"*I did not suffer, I am not suffering. The barriers I thought I had are not the barriers I thought they were. No blame here, no apportionment of blame - forgiveness.*"

(At this point I remembered my last letter, which, owing to his death, he did not receive. In it I had asked him what those barriers and blocks were, referred to by him in his previous letter!)

Dorothy continued:

It seems that he was surprised at the forgiveness he had received. He expected not to feel it. This is a soul who sounds as if he felt he needed forgiveness. He didn't, but he felt he did. He is looking right into your eyes.

"I am sorry. Forgive me," he says. He did not like himself, he did not like who he was. He has a lot of work to do, but he is finding healing. I can see a lot of healing around him. He is not a sad figure. He was, but he is no longer.

"I had to feel the pain I inflicted." He has been through the pain he inflicted on others, *"you included,"* he is telling you. He has to work in turn with all whom he inflicted with his brand of pain and to whom he caused hardship. He says, *"I was spiteful to the last, but that character does not belong to me now, and each in turn I will help."*

He has got two people with him now and he means the 'I' to include them. He is being helped to help people. *"My hand is in the work, and you will understand."* In the past he was in a position to help people and he didn't do it. He was a greedy man. *"I wanted to be punished but the punishment is love and that is harder. At my hands many suffered."*

Then Dorothy said a very strange thing:

He has just looked at me and said, *"The pain that I inflicted was the same pain that you went through."*

By "you" here, he seemed to mean Dorothy herself, but she said:

He did not inflict pain on me. He is just saying that, but he says he was the one who suffered in the end.

It is almost as if the love was too much for him to bear. *"I had to review myself. You can't get away from this, we all have to do it."* He is holding chains now as if he should be in chains, shackled. He is not shackled - he feels he should be. He is moving away from me now, Diana. I can't hold him any more. A lot of friendship.

"She was my guardian. Tell her I love her and that all losses will be made up."

The strange remark HL made to Dorothy - *"The pain that I inflicted was the same pain that you went through"* - took some unravelling between Dorothy and myself. She had no idea what he meant, so I asked her to tell me what 'pain' she had gone through. She told me how she and her husband had been harmed by someone who had cheated them out of their rights, and a great deal of money had been lost.

In return, I told her that HL had been involved in a somewhat similar situation, not by cheating, but by a failure in a family business. This failure seriously affected his close relatives. Up to this point I had not known Dorothy's story, and she had not known HL's. The only person who could possibly have known both versions was HL, and this only because he was in spirit and could see into her life. I feel sure that he made the remark to her in order that we would discuss it together and see it as positive proof of his presence with us in spirit. There was no need of proof for me, however. I had no doubt that it was HL speaking.

This meeting took place several months after Henri Leopold died. He did not receive the punishment he believed he deserved and which he had discussed so often with me on his visits to Topsham. I think it must have been quite hard for him to discard his hair shirt! I shall always remember him as the most caring Guardian that I am ever likely to find, and I value the (sometimes quite tough) arguments we used to have, but we both respected the other's beliefs and learned from all our discussions.

Several years after the death of HL I was up on Dartmoor on a few acres of land which I owned. It was fairly remote and I was alone cutting back the grass with a motor-driven scythe. I had been working for some time and the noise of the machine was getting me down, so I switched off the engine. I was rejoicing in the silence when I began to feel a sensation between my shoulder blades as if I were being watched. The sun was shining, the place was peaceful and I had no reason to feel apprehensive, but I did. It took some courage to turn slowly to confront whoever was looking at me. I expected to see some man who had come onto the land because of the noise of the machine, but it was not a man. About eight feet up the slope behind me stood a new-born fawn. He did not move when I turned. His big eyes were fixed upon me and we stared at each other for a little while. Then he began to wobble on his baby legs and slowly turned away and wandered off into the long grass.

I did not want to frighten him but I was interested to see where he had gone, so I followed the path he had taken, but could find no trace of him. It was only much later when I was writing this book that I recalled that Henri Leopold's code name when he was with the French Resistance was *Faune*. To those whose lives have been alerted to similar events this will be significant, a synchronicity, although to many it might appear to be a mere coincidence.

In Memoriam

I heard that when he died he left a note,
his dust to be interred beside the house
within the confines of that square of earth
no man could call a garden.

They emptied him amongst the bricks and stones
and raked him in as best they could that day,
and sighed as they surveyed the sorry scene;
yet one there was who cried and went away.

But they were wrong to see him in that place,
for he some days before had taken flight
to walk upon the solitary hills
above the sea-swept island that he loved -

if love's the word for one who made his home
a haven for his hoard to feed his need,
and consequently lived a hermit - prisoner of his greed
immersed in silence - but avoiding tax.

Yet love he did in spite of dogged Power
who, walking with him, stepping where he trod,
had even watched him fervent at the prayers
he murmured to a bureaucratic god.

I saw him once among the Standing Stones
upon the misted hill above the town;
he seemed to search for pockets in his shroud,
but in his spirit hands no cash was found,

just notes on pale pink paper, deeply scribed
with purple ink, which could not be erased.
And spreading each upon the stones he read,
words - which in life he constantly denied -

that he was loved.

Chapter 46

More About James Smeall

During the following years, with the help of others, I continued to run 'The Open Mind Group' in Topsham and this was a great help, for it kept my mind alert and helped me at a time when I was mourning the loss of Henri Leopold's investigative brain. Writing my book also took up a great deal of my time and James was, as always, a lively companion. We went on a number of holidays, to America, Rhodesia, Egypt and on a short cruise along the coast of Italy. James was a wonderful friend to travel with, apart from the times when he lost vital travel documents. Once he even tore up his air tickets as we crossed the Adriatic on our way home, and threw them merrily from the stern of the ship!

His ninetieth birthday in Topsham was a huge success. No invitations were sent out and yet about two hundred people turned up to his garden party! He made an excellent speech from the balcony of his house, the sun shone and his garden looked its best.

We were very close during this time. James had various health problems which he was inclined to dismiss as unimportant, but which I found disturbing. When the time came that he had to admit something was seriously wrong, he was indignant. He did not agree that it was his time to go, for he felt that he could last many more years. I don't think he ever really took in the seriousness of his condition right up until the last moment, but I was thankful that I was there to help him in order to repay him for all his generosity to me.

I went to Clare's for Christmas 1997, but was slightly worried that James was having difficulty using his left hand. However, he insisted that he was fine and I was only going for a few days. While I was away I had the first indication that I was seriously unwell myself, but when I returned, James' hand had become considerably worse, and he was now dragging his left foot as well. I understood that it was not likely to have been a mild stroke, as I had thought, but something far more serious. Later I discovered that the problem lay deep in his brain and that it was caused by at least one brain tumour.

From January onwards we made frequent visits to the hospital for his tests and X-rays. James was admitted to a ward but did not stay there very long. A few days later I drove him to the hospital again so that he could complete a course of X-rays, and wheeled him down to the department for an interview with the radiologist. The X-ray pictures showed clear evidence of the tumours. James asked how much longer he had to live. He was trying to give the impression that he was tough and could 'take it'. I knew he was not, but could not pass this information on to the radiologist while James was present, and so James was told in plain terms that he probably had six weeks.

This news seriously shook us both, although I had the advantage of having been warned that things were worse than we had anticipated. I wheeled him back to the ward to consider the various suggestions made by the doctor. He had been offered the possibility of radiotherapy, which might prolong his life by a few months, but which might also impair his brain. I suggested that we should discuss the future with the sister on the ward, who would have had much experience of the outcome of radiation on other patients. However, in true James fashion, it took him only a short time before he had convinced himself that the radiologist had said that his life span might be another five years, and he was content with that.

He returned home but was soon bedridden. This tried his patience and he was not the easiest person to nurse. I had to call his family and ask them to come down, and we managed to get some paid help, but not the professional nursing help which he was rapidly needing. Once his daughter was there, however, I had to leave the care of James to her. She was helped by her daughter and by the untrained nursing assistant. This was hard, for I was the one James wanted with him. As the days went by I realised that it was going to be impossible for him to remain at home without special care. He longed for me to take him back to my house but I could not have managed to nurse him there. The stairs were steep and, although he did not know it, I was not well myself.

I arrived one day to find him in a desperate state, weeping and very distressed at the position he was in. I talked to him about going to the local Hospice, and he was relieved at the thought. We therefore consulted his GP, who was very helpful, and James was taken into the Hospice that day. I cannot describe the relief of seeing him properly cared for in a clean bed.

From that moment onwards he returned to his old self and his final days were happy and peaceful. The only thing he missed was the company of his many friends, most of whom would have loved to have been with him, but his family allowed no visitors. However, I slept each night at the Hospice and was with him throughout his final days and nights whenever it was possible.

Towards the end of the final week my son-in-law came with me to see James before it was too late. We entered the ward in the evening and the night nurse asked if we were family. I told her that I was his girlfriend and had been with him every day since I had got him into the Hospice. She was concerned because she had been told that his family did not allow him to have visitors, but at that moment a loud voice boomed from the far side of the ward saying, "She's not my girlfriend! She's my LOVER!" and so there were no more objections.

The following day James was in great distress, and during the morning a male nurse came to see me in the waiting room and said that James was so restless and unhappy that it had been decided to give him a tranquilliser. The nurse felt that I should be there, as it was likely that James would not regain consciousness. It might be my last opportunity to say goodbye to him, as he was very near to death. I went back to the ward and sat with my arms round him while they gave him the injection. I was able to reassure him that I was with him and that I loved him, and to tell him that he would now sleep for a while. I knew that he had not taken any food for days and in the last twenty-four hours had had no water either. He simply did not have need of it, for his body was giving up. I remained close by and slept as usual at the Hospice during the following nights. He never recovered consciousness.

The Day of Fountains

Bandusian fountain cold and crystal clear
Worthy of tribute from the flocks you keep alive
when the dog-star rages darkly on the land.

A kid too young for lusts and fights will come
With flowers and holly to adorn your rocks.
The herdsman too will drink his thanks in wine.

Diana's fountain calms our own dog days,
The pebbled caverns cool and deep bring peace
The moon-deep tide of night will soon begin
And drowsy tinkling lead us into sleep.

James Smeall's adaptation of Horace's O Fons Bandusiae

On the 25th February 1998, James Smeall left this world and moved into a new life. (I was to learn about this change of dimension from his own description some nine months later). Early in the morning on the day before he officially died, I woke in my bed in the Hospice and felt that I must go to him. I went into the ward in my dressing gown and sat by his bed. At 6.30 that morning James took a deep breath and stopped breathing. I could not find a pulse, and gathered from his doctor later that it was at this moment that he suffered brain death.

After a little while, as I stayed beside him, I noticed that the sheet was moving very slightly over his diaphragm and I found that I could detect an occasional faint, erratic pulse. I felt sure that he had died, yet he lay like this throughout that day and the following night, by which time his body had stiffened in rigor mortis, yet the muscles of his heart still held tentatively onto life.

I was distressed and tired by the next morning, as I had spent many nights in the Hospice, and after speaking to the doctor and finding that James had been brain-dead since the morning of the day before, and that there was no possibility that he could regain consciousness, I decided to return to Topsham. Once home, I recorded a phone message to a priest who was a friend of ours and asked him to go to James as soon as he could, as he was somewhere between life and death but could not be certified as dead until his heart stopped.

Shortly after this I was rung up by another friend who asked, "Where is James? I must speak to him, because I have just had a very vivid dream about him." I told her that he was unconscious and dying in the Hospice. She did not know where that was, nor had she even known that he was ill. In her dream she had seen him standing by a wide series of windows in the centre of which was a glass door. James had his hand on the door handle and was about to go out into a garden when he turned and smiled at her. I told her that James' bed in the Hospice was beside a wide series of windows in the centre of which was a glass door opening out onto a garden.

I have been asked why it was not I who received this dream from him, but the answer is quite simple. If I had dreamt it, I would have failed to see its real importance. I knew where James was, knew he was dying, and was aware that his bed was beside the windows and the door seen in the dream, so I might have failed to realise that the dream was being given to me by James. The other friend, however, knew none of this and, after receiving the dream, felt urged to ring me up, probably prompted by James.

At midday Geoffrey Rowe, the priest I had phoned, happened to be visiting the main hospital. He had not been home and therefore had not received my message, but as he drove away from the hospital he suddenly decided to visit the Hospice and see how James was. He found him in a deep coma and near the point of death. He gave him a blessing and told him that it was time to go and that he should not hold on to his life any longer. Within a short while James' heart stopped, or as I might have said, James stopped his own heart!

A Sonnet to Wisdom

You left your wisdom floating in the air
and now it moves as motes in sunlight stray;
I kept the window closed to keep it there,
stilled in the night, but dancing through the day.
Such wisdom sometimes lurks above my head
I have no power to follow where you went.
I watch the road down which you came instead
to plant new thoughts before the dance is spent.
But time is slowly moving down the years
and you are gone, a memory fading fast;
yet, in the half-light sometimes there appears
faintest of forms returning from the past.
I sit and wait your coming if you will,
and if you will not, I am waiting still.

Chapter 47

26th February 1998 - Cancer

The day after James died, Adrian Renouf, my GP, came to see me early in the morning before breakfast. I was due to go to the surgical outpatient department at the Royal Devon and Exeter Hospital that morning for what was, I thought, a routine visit. He told me that he wanted someone to go with me. Clare and her husband Peter and their children had returned to their home to Suffolk and I did not feel it was necessary to bother anyone else. However he insisted, and I asked him if this meant that I had cancer. This rather embarrassed him and he said, "I did not say that."

I had been fairly certain ever since the previous New Year, that something serious was brewing, for I had experienced a really shattering pain during the night when I was baby-sitting in Newmarket for Clare, and I had been having investigations while James was ill. James' serious problems, accelerating as they did during January and February, eclipsed my symptoms and investigations, and I had no time to consider my own health. When, the day after James died, the surgeon told me that I had colon cancer it did not worry me. I was in a strange state of mind. Too many things had happened and I felt insulated against the news.

Things moved swiftly and, having had the cancer confirmed by X-rays, I was in the operating theatre within two weeks. All went well and I returned home after nine days to begin a long convalescence, during which I had time to take in the death of James. I was thankful that my own problems had not prevented me from caring for him during the seven weeks of the New Year when he was dying, and that I had been with him as he died. However, this did not seem to have prepared me for his absence when I returned home after my operation. It was hard to realise that he could not be with me at a time when I needed him so much.

Three months later I began the long drudge of chemotherapy, which was to go on every week until early in 1999. The Royal Devon and Exeter Oncology Department was excellent, and the sisters in charge did their best to make the treatment as trouble-free as possible, but unfortunately reaction against the drug used is inevitable because it poisons the system, and I began to feel deeply depressed.

In the Autumn of 1998, while still in the process of weekly chemotherapy, I had a long session with Dorothy Chitty. The first part of this meeting turned out to be most unexpected and a few moments after we sat down Dorothy indicated that she was in touch. She said that there were several men who wished to speak to me and she turned on the tape recorder. I had come hoping to meet James, but it was Hugh who was waiting for my arrival.

Dorothy spoke:

> There is a man here. He is giving you flowers, roses, and a wedding ring. He is wearing a blue uniform. He is telling you that part of his spirit has come forward into a grandchild. He says that you will know who this child is.

The tape recording of this interview is filled with interference, as always when there is a close spirit connection. It is hard to interpret and at this point the message became confused.

> Something he [Hugh?] wrote to you - poetry. He is so happy that you will be together more. He is saying:
>
> *"There were obstacles to our love but they made us all the stronger. We listened for a while but regret that we waited, but that is in the past now. It was true love. We are true to each other, we are one."*

I am sure this referred to my parent's objection to our friendship, which had meant that we had never been able to become engaged.

Dorothy continued the message which Hugh was giving her:

"This grandchild is spiritually aware. He will become a writer - he is very artistic. He has a love of words, he will seem at some stage in his life as if he is changing, but he will come back to it. He will be a writer. He will be successful in early years. The words that come through him are far beyond him and the meaning of them is beautiful. He is going to be recognised."

I told Dorothy that, in the last day or two one of my grandchildren had written a poem when he returned from school. He had written it at the kitchen table while my daughter was cooking supper and she was so impressed by it that she rang me up and read it to me. He was eight years old at the time.

WAR POEM

Guns rattling
People battling
Planes flying
People dying.

Bombs blowing
Bullets flowing
People fighting
Torches lighting.

Backs aching
Diggers making
Fighters killing
Graveyards filling.

War ends
World mends.

Written by a grandchild in 1998

The message from Hugh which referred to this child, came at a very appropriate moment. Not only had the child just written this poem, but when I rang my daughter to tell her about the message from Hugh, and how I believed it concerned her son, she told me how he had come home from school the day before, on the 11th November, after the school had had a two-minute silence during the morning. The children had been told to think of the soldiers killed in the First World War. My grandson explained to his mother that he had not done this, but had thought instead about "Granny Di's friend Hugh who had been killed in the Air Force in the Second World War." My daughter was surprised because she did not think he knew Hugh's name.

These three things, happening within forty-eight hours of each other, were deeply significant.

I had originally arranged this particular meeting with Dorothy Chitty in the hope that James Smeall would make contact with me. He had died in February that year and I was concerned for him for many reasons. He had not, in all the fourteen years of our close friendship, agreed with me on the subject of life after death, and in spite of his illness and the fact that he was over ninety when he died, he had had no wish to leave this life.

After a pause Dorothy began to speak:

> There is a man here. H is helping him to come forward. He is clearing his throat as if to draw attention to himself. This is the man you told me had recently died. He is saying that you did love him but not in the same way as he did, more as a friend......He loved a bit more than just as a friend. When he died he was surprised to go over so quickly. He is speaking to you.
>
> " I thought I would come back. I had the energy. I was concerned for the shock to you. I knew it would be a shock. You made me think, you made me laugh, we laughed together. More than that, you listened to me, we talked. You were my best friend.

*"I did not think it would be so bad - they are fighting together. I should have changed it, shouldn't I? I talked to you about it. **You told me.** What they are doing to each other saddens me. I cannot affect it, I cannot change it. They have to learn."*

James and I had discussed our wills some time before and I had suggested to him that it would be wise to leave something directly to his grandchildren, but he failed to do this. He was not prepared to face the prospect of his own death, and at the time the making or altering of wills seemed to bring it closer. Dorothy spoke again:

Dorothy: He has met up with a lady.

I asked whether it was James' wife, and she replied that it was.

James: *"I thought I would feel guilty but I didn't, that does not belong here, we leave that behind."*

After quite a long pause I asked for more information from James.

Dorothy: He says he is still here.

James: *"The first surprise for me was that I was told that I could not come back. That really surprised me and death itself, that surprised me. It was like waking from a dream, that the life I had had was the dream I had had. That's the way I can explain it. Everything was reversed. I am not sure that it all happened, yet I know it did.*

*I have come to a place that I cannot give a name to. It is a place of people. We don't have a body, we have a different **encasement**.* [Dorothy found this word hard to understand].

I brought my memory with me. I am now far more in touch with my memory than I ever was before. We go to a place of healing. That is where I found myself first, and the love that I was presented with was almost overwhelming in its effect on me. It was only afterwards that I realised that I expected this love. The presence of who you call 'God' is here, the presence is everywhere.

It wasn't a question that I don't believe. Once I was here that question no longer existed. The beauty that is here is beyond Earth's dimension. I can only thank you for prising my eyes open a little. You opened my heart and prised my eyes open to what the possibilities were.

In this place, which is another world, I have seen members of my family which go back to the beginning of my memory in the last lifetime and the one before. It isn't a place that is crowded: they do move on. There are energy bands, different life atmospheres, but they are energies and apparently as we progress we go into another energy. The way for us to progress is to help those of you who are left behind. That is how it seems - you are left behind, we are the ones travelling forward. Excitement is not the word, it is acceptance. I had to face myself and my death. That wasn't easy. I had a review of my life which wasn't easy - not a finger-pointing exercise you understand - a review of what I did and did not do, how I stood back and did or did not behave. There is something called Karma. Karma is written here. Karma is an energy that is written which goes far beyond comprehension.

It does seem funny that I can hear conversations with you - can go back into the past and hear your frustration with me. My understanding is that you and I were each other's challenge - not confrontation, you understand, but challenge. I used to think I could make you change your mind, and you used to think that you could make me change mine. In our ways we were both stubborn and both strong in our beliefs - or unbeliefs, on my part.

This journey is truly beautiful. At first I did not know that I had died. I thought I was waking up from a dream, thinking I was still at home in my own bed. Because our thoughts stay with us, we can still think. Our thoughts are not judgemental. I think I felt like arguing and saying I AM NOT DEAD. I was told then, 'You are not dead...you have created a new life. Death is not death, death is the ending of the mortal body. It is the beginning of the continual journey of the spiritual body.'

Don't I sound knowledgeable!!!

The healing is instantaneous here. Do you know there is no such thing as time here? Time is now, time was so important to me before. I am still myself, but so different. For all those whom we used to term unbelievers, those who are as stubborn as I was - don't worry about them. What we used to call the mortal soul - there is no such thing. The soul is Soul, purity. We used to discuss about people who had done terrible things: there is a place for all here. Remember how I told you that I had to face my life? We all have to do the same, every one of us, and then we have to work our way out, earn our way out. It can sometimes take what we might have called a lifetime, in what was our time. There are beings, and we recognise them, beings known in history books who have created atrocities. We can view them but we do not have to mix with them.

I am tired now. I will speak with you again. There are gardens here. Things are different, things are done by thought.

I still love you, my dear friend. Thank you for our..."

At this point James blew me a very spectacular kiss!

Later at the same meeting, Dorothy told me that there was another man waiting to speak to me. This man's name began with F. It has taken me some time to realise why, when in contact with spirits, only the first letter of the name by which they are known is usually given. It is rare for a whole name to be used. I think this is because the use of symbols is a common means of communication.

The man came forward into Dorothy's vision. I told Dorothy that I could not place him and she said she would ask him to identify himself. She told me that he was a man from quite a long way in the past. On further thought I suddenly wondered if it could be my father (who, it will be remembered, was a doctor) but I did not say so to Dorothy.

A few minutes later Dorothy said:

This is a doctor in spirit, a medical doctor. He is showing me a white coat. He is saying that he is proud of you. He is saying that you are a *"chip off the old block."* [Very typical of my father!] He says, *"She has the same integrity."* He thought at one time that you would follow in his footsteps. *"I didn't bargain with her having such a strong mind of her own."*

Dorothy said to me at this point, "You must have done something like that...some sort of healing?"and I told her that I had indeed been very interested in absent healing and consultations towards healing.

> Dorothy: He is patting you on the back and blowing a kiss to you. He says your mother is here. She is saying that she was an iron fist in a velvet glove - she seemed soft and gentle but was strong inside.

It was at this point Hugh returned with James and I was not able to continue the conversation with my mother which I would have liked to do. I was amazed that my parents had come forward like this, because they were not interested in spiritual things and were almost afraid of anything psychic. I would have liked to have spoken with my brother Peter, who had died all those years ago, and who would, I am sure, have been in touch with my mother.

The presence of my parents had a different feeling to that which dominated the meetings with other close friends. They seemed more distant, more like strangers who were pleased to catch up with me for a moment. Later on I had a very strong conviction that they had wanted to explain why they had prevented me from seeing Hugh, and was very certain that somewhere on this tape I would find the passage where they explained this. I was amazed, however, on re-running it, to find that this explanation was not there.

Chapter 48

Absent-clairvoyance

Early in 1999 my course of chemotherapy ended and I decided to sell 48 The Strand, leave Topsham, and go to Suffolk to be nearer to my daughter Clare and her family. Once the sale of the house had gone through, however, I woke up one morning with an urgent feeling that I should also buy a flat in Topsham. I knew that I would not be happy without a foothold in the town after all the years I had been there, and so that very day, straight away, I went up Fore Street to Paul Property Services, the office of a company which dealt in local property.

As I reached the door of the office, a young woman entered ahead of me. She approached the desk and said that she wanted to sell her flat in the town, as she was interested in buying a smaller one. Acting on my psychic instinct, I stopped her in her tracks and said that I would be interested in buying her flat. It transpired that the agents had just the flat *she* wanted already on their books, so the deal went through swiftly and I became the owner of 7 Kenyon Court, a two-bedroomed flat facing south, in the centre of the town. Leaving my new flat in the hands of Paul Property, who found someone to rent it immediately, I left Topsham after twenty-nine years, feeling that, should my health improve sufficiently, I still had the possibility to return and had not burned my boats completely.

I moved to Suffolk and began living in a cottage on property belonging to Clare and her husband Peter. It was a barn I had had renovated and was very attractive, but even so I began to feel that I had made a wrong decision. It had probably been unwise to make such a drastic move when still under the influence of chemotherapy and its side effects, but at the time I was deeply depressed and fairly certain that I had not much longer to live. However, this proved to be quite untrue.

While I was at the cottage in Lidgate, I wanted to resume my previous contact with those in spirit who had added so much to my life in the past, but I knew of no clairvoyants in Suffolk. I remembered one person in Essex who had psychic experience, and when I telephoned him for some advice, he very kindly gave me the telephone number of a contact of his who, he felt sure, would be able to help. I rang the number he had given me without knowing the name of the person to whom I was about to speak, and the man who answered gave me the phone number of another man called Ray Bayley who practised absent-clairvoyance and who lived in the Midlands. In the light of what was to happen later, it was important that there was no possibility that anyone could have given Mr Bayley any information about me. I did not realise the significance of this at the time, however.

When I spoke to Mr Bayley, he asked me to send him a blank sheet of paper, touched by no-one other than me, on which I had written my name, age and address and anything else I wanted him to know.

That evening I took paper from a new computer pack, wrote my name, age and address on it, placed the sheet on the back of an antique table in my sitting room so as to be certain that it was not touched by anyone else, and I posted it the following morning to Mr Bayley. I had been told not to expect a reply for a week or two. I would then receive an audio tape-recording of the result of the spirit session Mr Bayley would have had while holding my paper in his hands.

The tape arrived as expected, but turned out to be totally different from what I had anticipated. Mr Bayley had had remarkable success with my blank paper, and although the tape was not easy to follow and was very involved, I will try to record those parts which were significant. The incidents on the tape were hard to decipher and there were, of course, no dates to enable one to follow the sequence, but I could easily select those parts which I knew to be accurate and from these I was able to get the whole picture.

After mentioning various names which I could not place, Ray

finally came up with the name 'Kitty' which he felt might be the name of my grandmother. I was encouraged by this, for although the name of one of my grandmothers was Christine, she had always been known as Kitty. Ray also mentioned another woman whom he thought might be my mother because of her age. He saw the two women and me connected with a very unusual table. At the same time he picked up the name of 'Byron' whom he believed to have been a poet living on an island off Italy. This information was astounding as it was very significant. He went on to see a castle and asked if there was a castle in the family.

Ray then said, "This is a story and a very important story," and told me that he had contacted a man who worked in the City of London at the beginning of the century. He thought that the man had been a banker, and that he was interested in quality antiques, a collector. "I can see an important table, antique, probably Chippendale, mahogany colour. There was a huge house in a Georgian square linked to Kitty. I can see a young boy who passed tragically at the age of seven, a sudden death, a close family link causing much sorrow."

The information in the last paragraph came through in a very disjointed way and has been collected together from the tape by me. Ray told me that there was a man, perhaps my father, who was regretful of events in the past. This man wanted me to know that what he and my mother had done (when they had tried to prevent my meetings with Hugh just before his death) they did because they thought it was all for the best. This reminded me of the meeting with Dorothy Chitty some years before, when I had felt sure that my father had wanted to say this, and had been so surprised not to find a record of it on the tape she gave me at the time. That my father should return through a different clairvoyant at a later date and complete what he had been unable to say before, was remarkable. This part of my contact with Ray makes it clear that spirits appear not at the request of the medium, but because of the need of the client.

The following letter to Ray explains all that was significant on the tape and clarifies most of the extremely detailed and important connections which he had picked up from the paper I sent him:

13th March 2001

Dear Mr Bayley,

Thank you very much for the tape. It contained some extraordinary contacts which I had not expected and it dealt with quite a different part of my life from the meetings I have had with Dorothy Chitty, my clairvoyant in Devon. There were, of course, a number of things I could not place, but there were far more which made sense. I will go through it from the notes I made as I listened to the tape for the second time.

You mention my mother, and probably her mother, as being involved in a very unusual story, and you give me the name 'Kitty' as possibly being the name of my grandmother. You were right, she was named Christine but was always called Kitty. You mention 'Byron'(?) a poet who lived on an island off Italy, being closely involved in the story, and you also refer to an unusual antique table, owned by my family. The name was in fact Browning, Robert Browning, the poet, who lived for a time in Venice. There is a definite connection between him and my grandparents.

The banker or financier who you saw living in London at the beginning of the last century, 'who was a collector of antiques,' was my grandfather, my mother's father, Norman Herbert Smith, who founded a company of solicitors in the City of London at the beginning of the last century. He, as he showed you, collected beautiful furniture, Sheraton and Chippendale, and particularly one special table *which has since been handed down through the family. He was the solicitor who sorted out the Browning inheritance in 1907, at which time the daughter-in-law, Mrs Browning, who had inherited all the Browning effects at the death of her husband, Robert Browning's only son, gave my grandfather this very rare supper table, which had been the property of Elizabeth and Robert Browning. This table has always been known in the family as 'the Browning Table' and has been greatly treasured. I think you might easily have heard the poet's name Browning as 'Byron' in the circumstances.*
The table came to my mother after her mother, Kitty, died, and

*later it was left to me. It was beside me as I wrote to you and the
sheet of paper I sent to you rested on this table during the night
before it was posted. I find all this quite amazing. I wonder
whether the table could have influenced the paper which lay
upon it during the night? If so, it is of great importance. Your
instructions that the paper should not be touched by anyone
else, did not seem to me to concern the table. Have you come
across such a thing happening before?*

*The young boy you mention, who died unexpectedly, was my
brother. He was seven years old at the time of his death and I,
aged three, adored him. He died tragically in twenty-four
hours in 1924, from what was thought to be pneumonia. He
was my parents' eldest child and their only boy at the time. A
year after his death I was in our house in London and I met him
in the nursery passage. It was a grey London evening, and the
lights were not yet on. He walked towards me, smiled and
waved his hand.*

*The two people mentioned at the end of the tape are my mother
and father who prevented Hugh, my fiancé, and myself from
getting officially engaged, and tried to stop us seeing each
other. He was killed in the Battle of Britain in 1940. I think
that this is why you see them as regretful, but they felt that
they were doing the right thing at the time. The link with the
sea is from my great-great-grandfather, who was a sea captain
and was the Harbour Master of Padstow in Cornwall. Our
family was also connected with a castle in Wales but that
passed on to another branch of my ancestors.*

*So you see there was a great deal of important material on the
tape and your ability to see it as a "very important story" was
correct. They say that walls have ears: I begin to wonder
whether tables have memories!*

*With very many thanks for all the trouble you have taken, and
hoping to hear from you.*

All this from the new sheet of A4 computer paper which I sent to
him, on which was written nothing but my name, address and age!

I am seriously interested in the possibility that information was
picked up from the table. We know that many people are able to gather

information from other inanimate objects, such as pieces of jewellery, and Ray himself was picking up everything from a sheet of paper, so why might a table not 'remember' its owners, makers, and those who have cared for it over the centuries? Why might it not imprint this knowledge onto a sheet of paper which lies upon it and then comes into the hands of a medium?

Ray Bayley was fascinated at the suggestion that my remarkable table might have had a hand in passing on the information about the poet, Robert Browning, and his ownership of it. The table itself is worth describing here as it is very beautiful. It is a circular supper table, made in about 1760 and carved all round on the outer edge with large scallop shells in which small dishes can be placed. The pedestal is carved with acanthus leaves and the three feet are decorated with claws holding a ball. They are not the usual lion's claws, but longer, finer, bird's claws. This carving was done some time after the table was made, in the early part of the nineteenth century. The whole story is extraordinary and has increased my affection for this beautiful and useful object.

Return to Topsham

During the next two years in Suffolk my depression refused to go away and I finally realised that the answer was staring me in the face. I had only to repossess my flat and I could return to Topsham and all my friends. At that precise moment I received a letter from Paul Property Services telling me that the tenants who were renting the flat had given notice to leave. The decision was made for me.

In the following months I arranged for painters, carpenters and plumbers to invade the flat and I went down to Topsham myself on one or two occasions to see their progress. All went well and I was able to move in October 2001. My return was a joy to me, and every expedition down Topsham's main street took an age: even buying a loaf of bread required at least half an hour as I chatted with the many friends who stopped me and seemed delighted that I had returned. My depression vanished, my computer cried out for some exercise, and the chapters of this book began to cover the table, the chairs and the floor.

Occasionally I see the shadow of James striding towards the pub at lunchtime and think how wonderful it would be if things had been different. But things are as they are. We have no control over the pattern of our lives, only over the way in which we carry the pain or welcome the joy.

Chapter 49

Tides of Life

So much water has gone under the bridge since I first set out to put my life into words, that I feel I need to tie together some of the events which have occurred over my eighty-five years. I am particularly interested in bringing together those experiences which have been life-changing. My first introduction to such an experience was when I met my brother a year after he had died. I was only four years old, but the meeting has had a lasting effect upon me.

The next deeply affecting event happened when I was nineteen, in August 1939. Through a repeated dream, I became aware that someone was coming to meet me and that the meeting would take place within the next few weeks. When I met Hugh Haswell a fortnight later, I knew immediately that he was the person I had been expecting. This was certainly a life-changing event, and was followed within the year by an even more dramatic dream concerning an event which, tragically, changed my life for ever.

This second dream, in which I saw myself being married to someone other than Hugh, involved precognition and also, indirectly, told of his death. It took place eleven months after I met him, on the night of the 25th July 1940. Earlier that day, unknown to me, he had been recorded as 'Missing', and had in fact been killed. The precognitive aspect of the dream was acted out some years later at the time of my marriage. The strange thing is that the dream did not, in fact, tell me of Hugh's death, only of my eventual marriage, and yet I knew without any doubt whatsoever that Hugh was telling me he was dead. Indeed, two days before he was known by me to be 'missing', I told a friend that he was dead. That he could enable me to have this dream after he had left this life, was proof that the word 'death' had a totally different meaning within the timelessness of his new existence.

Dreams of precognition are not usually looked on as warnings, more as information about the time we conceive of as 'the future', information which will only be understood after the event. In connection with the later dream which took place on a railway station, I decided on waking *not* to make the journey as planned, but this initial decision was then changed by me. Had I not changed my mind in this way the dream could not have occurred. It is important to realise this: precognition only shows events which *do* occur. It was, I believe, in the knowledge of the giver of the dream that this event would lead to the break-up of my marriage, something which turned out to be a necessary move in the future.

The strange experience I had at Inyanga was rather different. It took place in timelessness, was immediate, and could not be explained. However, within a short period it also revealed itself as life-changing, and has been the hub of the wheel of my life ever since. I would hesitate to try to identify the Source through which this experience was given, for some things cannot be put into words. Many years later, however, the 'knowing' was translated into words by the exceptional medium George Pratt, when he spoke in a trance. When I heard what he said I was instantly aware that I had heard those very words long, long before in the mountains of Inyanga.

The saving of little David's life was so strange that I can only guess at how it happened. It was one of those occasions when time stops and you are taken under control by an unknown power. I have a clear memory of the moment before the control began, and again of the time when it stopped, but of nothing in between. I can also now connect this event with a much later moment when the name 'David' was given to me by a medium relaying a message from Hugh. Connections of this sort are convincing for they often clarify something which has been at the back of one's mind for a long time.

On the occasion of the saving of the life of the second child, when I woke Robert in the night, I knew that I was being used as a means of conveying a message. I had been woken by my voice speaking in words which did not come from my own mind. There was never any doubt about this at the time. Only in retrospect did I discover that the saving of David's life was almost certainly directed by Hugh, and the saving of the second child probably by one of the child's own relatives, also working from another dimension.

Other experiences have been quite different. When, as a tiny child, I met my brother in the nursery passage more than a year after he had died, I knew he was Peter by the way he was revealed to me; he was not a ghost. Similarly, when my brother-in-law came into my bedroom twenty-four hours after he died, he came dressed in a kilt, recognisably in the tartan of the London Scottish. He had been a sad, shrunken corpse the night before and was now at his best, healthy and young. On both these occasions communication took place wordlessly and recognition was immediate.

The meeting with Bes, the dwarf, was different again. I could not recognise him, for he was unknown to me. It did not strike me at the time that it was odd for a dwarf to come into the room when I was in hospital in labour. He took control of my mind, and maybe of my body too, for he took away the pain of the second stage of labour. The help given to me by Bes could not be recalled in words, for none of it was spoken, but passed from mind to mind in pain relief and 'knowing'.

A similarity between the psychic events which I have included here, is that they were all partly conducted in timeless zones, but of the six major reunions I have had with friends and family who have died, most occurred during meetings with a medium and were therefore psychic events of a very different sort. They are included in this book in detail from tapes made at the time, and I feel I need to describe the way in which they related to each other. There were many different reasons why each person appeared. My first contact was with Hugh, who came wearing blue and identified himself to the medium as my husband. When I told her that this was not so, she said that he had always considered this to be so. In response to a question from the medium, he described how his death had occurred - facts which were unknown to anyone, including me. He was aware of my need to know the facts of his dying and came through the medium initially for that reason. From that time onwards he came back in many different ways during the succeeding years.

The appearance of Jean was also necessary for her and for her family, because she had died traumatically and knew that those who loved her were deeply worried. When she came forward I was not sure who she was and had to ask for a description of her death in order to identify her, as I had also done in Hugh's case. Jean communicated clearly in spite of the short time since her death, which sometimes impedes the ability of spirits to make contact. The circumstances of her dying were dramatically described by the medium who had no previous knowledge of it whatsoever. The inclusion of the detail of a fruit cake on her tea table during one of the scenes, was the symbol by which her sisters were convinced that it was Jean herself speaking. This symbol could not have been interpreted by anyone other than her sisters. Similarly, in the case of Norman Yendell, when he realised that I had not been able to identify him through his offering of olive wood, he immediately made the sound of his hammer and chisel on wood, at which I recognised him as a sculptor and a close friend. The use of symbols on both of these occasions is remarkably convincing.

Henri Leopold's return was extraordinary. There was no way that I could have mistaken him for anyone else, in spite of the fact that he appeared with no identification apart from his chained hands. After the long series of letters from him on the subject of purgatory, he must have known that my immediate reaction would be one of horror and disbelief, for I had been convinced that after death he would find only love. When he parted his hands to show that he was not chained, I realised that the chains were symbolic, and that without their use there was no way in which he could have shown me that he was free of his vision of purgatory.

None of the appearances which came through Dorothy Chitty were 'seen' by me, only recognised from her descriptions, and it was therefore necessary for those returning to make themselves known by showing recognisable symbols. This was very clear when my father came unexpectedly. I did not recognise him from Dorothy's description until he had shown her a white coat, which she recognised as belonging to a doctor. He came to tell me how proud my parents were of me and that my mother was there with him, at which point he was overtaken by the appearance of another arrival, but some years later, when I was in touch with a different medium, he returned and completed what he had been going to say.

This is interesting, as it is an example of contact with a spirit who seems to need to find a way to come back in order to ask for forgiveness. It was surprising to me that my father could connect with me on a different occasion, through another medium, in order to explain the reason why he and my mother behaved as they did, and to ask for forgiveness. This links with the meeting with James who, when he returned, explained to me that he had been told that in order to progress, he had to put right the problems he had left behind, and the pain which he felt he had caused in this life.

The years spent with Henri Leopold in which we were 'guardians' of each other were, in themselves, life-changing for both of us. His account of the dream he had during the night before his death was, I am certain, written for me. In it he saw his mother and father pass his bedroom door in their night-clothes, but he did not take this as an omen. He enjoyed dreaming and spent much time analysing the meaning of dreams, but I would not have said that he was a psychic. However, he was a willing listener to my accounts of the psychic and spiritual events which arose in my life, and always suggested helpful and positive interpretations. I owe him a great deal for his return after death in order to remove my deep concern about him, and to complete his chapter in this book.

James Smeall has also taken up quite a number of pages towards the end of this book. It became apparent, as he spoke through Dorothy, that one of the reasons for his return was his need to help me. He had been shown this by those who helped him to review his own life. He knew that the best way he could offer his help was to describe his new life, and the location in which he found himself, as all this would be of the utmost importance to me. To him also I owe a great debt of gratitude for his return.

There is little to add to my account of Ray Bayley's fascinating tape-recording, which was made *in absentia* with nothing but a sheet of paper written on by me. The power involved in such readings is quite beyond me. I do not know whether I believe that the table itself was able to bring forward so much information, but I begin to wonder whether it is possible that the spirit within the life of the tree, from which the table was made, could retain memories. We are not surprised when places and houses have psychic atmosphere, so I can see no reason why wood should not also harbour spirit memories. Research into events such as this could be very rewarding.

Our deepest feelings of love and loss bring us into touch with those who have been closest to us both in life and death, and as our minds expand with the development of psychic knowledge, we are forced to consider the unexplained. I believe that some of us are given lives in which to discover more about the power of the Spirit. Through music, art and poetry, and through science, we capture beauty, and beauty is indeed truth if we see with Keats' eyes. These gifts are not confined to religions, to the churches, temples or any other places of worship. Very often it has been through the arts that people of all beliefs of this world have sought to portray personal longing for something 'other than'. This seeking suggests a soul-hunger for the 'All That Is', a longing which lies hidden deep within each one of us.

Raynor Johnson, a well known psychic, says in his book *The Imprisoned Splendour*:

No man, however distinguished be the quality of his mind, and however good his technique, can say "I will now sit down and write a great poem, or compose a great symphony, or make an important discovery." There is a level deeper than Mind from which all inspirations and all creative insights arise...

He continues by stating that when

...not by thought or by cogitation, one has a completely convincing fact of immediate experience, *this is a mystical experience...*

By the phrase "completely convincing fact of immediate experience" he seems to mean a state of insight not derived through the Mind, and not yet formulated in words. This idea of insight is expressed by Robert Browning in his poem *Paracelsus:*

Truth is within ourselves,
It takes no rise from outward things...
Rather consists in opening out a way
Whence the imprisoned splendour may escape,
Than in effecting entry for a light
Supposed to be without.

In a mystical experience we lose our sense of self and receive that which comes as a 'knowing' without words, and the memory stays with us to the end of our lives and beyond. In dreams we frequently receive the same 'knowing,' and even when we are unable to recall the details of the dream it has still entered into the depths of our memory. It was through a dream which I could not recall that I was enabled to use my computer to create the following poem. I closed my eyes and placed my hands on the keyboard, allowing my mind to control the action of my fingers without thought, and the following words were born in the form of prose without any punctuation. I was then able to order them into the poem set out below. The poem seemed to be given as a revelation and led me forward into a new chapter in my spiritual life.

The Dream of the Pool

I searched for the Self,
which is beyond all searching,
in the depths of a pool left in the rocks
by the receding ocean;
there, in that pool, a reflection of self.
I spoke to the pool and asked it who it was.

"Are you the ocean which formed you,
the rocks which surround you,
the sunlight which reflects in you,
the creatures which live in you?
Or are you water which lies
in a hollow of rock?"
The pool answered me.
"Wait and watch."

In the long waiting I watched the pool,
I watched the ocean,
I became pool in my understanding.
I felt the reflection of sun,
the movement of creatures in the depths.
I became the coolness of water,
the hardness of rocks,
and I waited.

Time passed.
Ocean crept upon the rocks,
in the darkness of night it overcame pool,
reclaiming that of itself
left amongst rocks on the falling tide.
Pool returned to Ocean exulting, free,
carrying experience into the All
known before birth, one with Ocean,
the All That Is. Yet I, on the dry rocks,
waited and watched.

As dawn broke over the Earth
Ocean receded, pool formed, water in rock.
I said "This is my self, I am this pool,"
but the pool said,
"Wait, watch and listen".

"I am no separate pool. I, an aspect of Ocean,
shall be taken and again made free.
Tide which formed me will reclaim me,
rocks, which gave me form,
will hold a new aspect of Ocean.
That which you have named pool
is form filled by Ocean."

"Consider the reality of pool,
that which is All That Is,
ever changing, ever the same,
past thoughts now one with Ocean.
Born today, a new form of Ocean,
new thoughts on the falling tide
in the evening of time."

I was afraid, I saw myself
without form, an emptiness.
I no longer knew whether I was.
Was I space within the form of my flesh?
Was I no thing, incomprehensible?

Wisdom from Ocean claimed my mind.
"You, ever changing, yet always the same.
As pool desires Ocean, you desire All That Is
into Whom you will be taken,
on the turn of the tide."